Satan

Get out in the name of

Jesus

An Autobiographical Account of a Personal Struggle Against Demonic Forces of Darkness

Marie Lynn

Dedication

To Jesus Christ, my Lord and Savior,
who has never turned away from me despite my rebellion. I
also dedicate this book to my family, who have stayed strong
in spite of the enemy; to my father, who would have given
me the world if only he were able; to my mother, who gave
birth to me; to my mother-in law, who has answered my late-
night phone calls and stepped in when my mother was
unable; to my father-in-law, who has provided reassurance
and guidance through his ministry; to my husband, who loves
me no matter how my world has turned upside down; and to
my sister, who has been my closest ally.

About the Author

Raised in a family shaped by unique challenges, this author discovered a deep passion for the Arts at an early age. Despite growing up with a schizophrenic mother, she found solace in creative expression and pursued higher education, eventually earning both a bachelor's and master's degree.

As a dedicated elementary school teacher, she brings creativity into the classroom. As a survivor of a demonic attack, her personal journey has led her to incorporate sermons, Scripture, and Christian music into her daily life as part of her healing process. She is an active Christian, singing in the church choir and teaching Sunday School, where her love for God and others shines.

An artist at heart, she enjoys painting in a variety of mediums, believing that art helps us process our experiences and reveals the depths of our inner world. A nature enthusiast, she also finds inspiration outdoors, creating nature-themed art that reflects her love for the beauty and tranquility of the natural world.

Throughout her life, this author has remained a passionate learner, always seeking to grow both personally and spiritually. Her experiences, whether teaching, creating art, or overcoming adversity, have shaped her into a compassionate and insightful individual who continually strives to deepen her understanding of herself and the world around her.

Table of Content

Preface

You can rebuke Satan by giving him commands like "Come out in the name of Jesus Christ," and you can plead the shed blood in the name of Jesus Christ but negotiating with Satan is simply not possible. You might think that he is capable of empathizing with you as you express your deepest sorrows and tears roll down your face; however, Satan is a master of manipulation and deception, and *"The thief comes only to steal and kill and destroy; [Jesus has] come that they may have life, and have it to the full"* (John 10:10, NIV). Satan is not known for listening with compassion and was thrown out of Heaven for leading a rebellion against God. *"Be alert and of sober mind. Your enemy the devil prowls around like a roaring lion looking for someone to devour"* (1 Peter 5:8, NIV).

This book is a glimpse into my life from my youth until now, growing up through trying times, transitioning into adulthood, and battling demonic forces while just trying to get by. My story is for some but not all. In places, I share graphic details and expose the sin in my life in a way that most people will find uncomfortable to read. I describe demonic and heavenly forces that require the recognition that magic is real. I intend to bring awareness and hope to all who encounter the enemy by sharing my personal struggles, revelations, and successes against the enemy, along with knowledge of Jesus Christ, who made my victories possible by paying the price for my sin and defeating my enemy. The people in my story are anonymous. Instead of naming them with pseudonyms, they have been left unnamed to help retain the authenticity of my story. Some of the events that occurred may be slightly out of order because they have become part of one enormous, timeless experience in my mind. My personal artwork is scattered throughout. Some, if not all, of my artwork may have been influenced by demonic forces. Many of my paintings are revelatory, having been painted before I became aware of the demonic influences in my life, yet they reveal so much of what I would encounter later in life.

As I deep-dive into discoveries from researching, I broadly discuss the topic of Kabbalah. It is not my intention to teach Kabbalah. I have not been formally instructed in it, and my beliefs and declarations are speculative. The study of Kabbalah is reserved for a select group of males at least 40 years of age, but it is my understanding that this is not enforced. My knowledge of Kabbalah has been pieced together from my personal experience as a victim of what I believe to be Kabbalah magic and from numerous sources of literature and videos. Kabbalah is an esoteric practice with roots in Judaism, not a religion itself, and is practiced by a number of religious orders and organizations. There are a variety of traditions of Kabbalah and a variety of spellings for the word. These traditions have similarities and differences. I will not distinguish between traditions because I do not specialize in any of them, nor do I intend to.

I have been telling Satan to leave me for several years now, but his spirits still work around the clock to torment me. When all is well, and my faith is strong, I barely feel them faintly poking or moving on the surface of my skin. In moments of defeat, depression, or doubt, the sensations intensify and can become overwhelming. When spirits enter, it feels as though a gust of wind is forcing its way past a barrier guarding the entrance to my ear canal.

This is usually accompanied by an itch on my backside. I feel the itch and then the gust. It is as if the itch is a knock on my door, and by thinking of it, I am granting permission for the spirit to come in. This happens so quickly that I cannot consciously decide to ignore the itch. Spirits never seem to exit through the ear but instead come out through a cough or sneeze. Whenever I feel a spirit moving within me, I must batten down the hatches and go into intense spiritual warfare. Prayer gets me through it all.

Jesus gives us the authority to cast out demons in his name: *"And these signs shall follow them that believe; In my name shall they cast out devils…"* (Mark 16, NIV). I was able to evict the lust spirit in this manner. Just like all other spirits, it can be difficult to recognize. Lust is something that can come over us, but we do not typically attribute it to an unclean spirit. We tell ourselves it is just how we are feeling and then search for a way to express it. I was only aware that it was the lust spirit because I have been battling unclean spirits that have been attempting to sexually assault me for at least four years. I am more suspicious of and resistant to sexual impulses than I ever was before this experience. When the lust spirit entered, I was completely disinterested in sex, yet I felt as though I was being aroused. I commanded the spirit to leave in the name of Jesus with faith, and it fled, freeing me from its grasp. As it left, I felt a sense of relief and victory. There is genuine power in the name of Jesus.

The spirit had come in during a lucid dream. Satan can attack us even in our sleep. Several times, I have woken up from what might be called a wet dream. I am in an unfamiliar place with unfamiliar people, and then a dark-haired, mysterious person approaches. As soon as this happens, I begin to feel throbbing, and if I allow it for even a second, I wake up fully aroused with what I believe to be an incubus spirit at work. Although the details of the dream are hazy, I remember being on a colorful, rainbow-themed carousel swing. As I spun around in circles, the seat gently stimulated me, creating a sensation that I would rather forget. In the dream, I asked what it was called and was told it was "rainbow puss." At the time, the name did not mean anything to me, but after waking up and battling the incubus spirit, I realized that the name was inappropriate and that I was being demonically attacked during my lucid dreams. I have had this type of dream several times.

I have woken up answering questions that clearly came from the enemy. "Why would you want to stay in this wasteland anyway?" My answer is because I do not believe this is a wasteland. I believe that every day is a gift, and I want to accomplish what God has intended for me. Another morning, I heard what sounded like a witch's voice telling me, "You hate him and his son." If the enemy feels it is necessary to come against my faith in Jesus Christ, then my faith in Jesus must be my strength. I have also woken up speaking curses against myself that came through my mind but were not my thoughts or words: "I place poison on my eyes and have blindness." When this happens, I immediately plead the shed blood of Jesus to cancel the curses.

On August 3rd, 2024, I was threatened by a demon that tapped the right side of my forehead and sent the message, "I deliver beautiful flowers to your obituary." When I heard this, I pled the shed blood of Jesus over my life and my family forever. Each morning, I plead the shed blood of Jesus over my family, myself, God's people, and all those God wills to save. I often do the same before I go to bed. I am blessed to know that there is power in the blood of Jesus and that despite what the enemy wants me to believe, God loves me and all his people.

Although I am still battling spirits, I have learned to trust in God, knowing that God is always with me and not to let fear take hold. Whenever fear has taken hold, I find myself overwhelmed by demonic attacks. Like a spider numbing its prey, I feel a deadly bliss as the sensations of touch grow stronger. Left unchecked, they become sexual and all-consuming. I have worked hard to get free from these attacks to the point that I barely feel the invisible touch and am able to function fully, but the credit for my victory goes to Jesus, who made this possible because it is only in his name that I have found deliverance and peace from the enemy. My weapons are prayer and faith in my Heavenly Father. The Lord strengthens me in my weakness, for his *"Power is made perfect in weakness"* (2 Corinthians 12:9, NIV).

There are people who believe that sexual union is the way to salvation. Some Kabbalists initiate this attack on women in an attempt to actualize with their souls, and many of the women who are their victims have been deceived into believing that they are experiencing their twin flame, divinely orchestrated by God, to help them grow spiritually. The women believe they will ascend in union with their twin flame, the complementary half of their soul, restoring their soul's wholeness and unity. This is the demonic attack I have been battling, and these beliefs are lies.

The Kabbalists seek to use the souls of the many women to achieve their "Great Work." No partnership exists in this relationship; rather, this is more like a parasitic relationship. The soul material of the women is purified into silver through alchemical transmutation performed by the Kabbalist, which is then combined with his own transmuted soul material, which has become gold. The souls come together through alchemical marriage to give birth to a perfected soul, which will serve as the vehicle for the Kabbalist to enter on his quest for enlightenment.

The spirits of the women, who are then disrobed without a soul of their own, are sometimes referred to as virgin spirits or white garments in some literature. They are interconnected as Sephiroth along the Lightning Path on the Tree of Life. They will be used as batteries and transformers to step down powerful, divine energy to the Kabbalist on his quest to become a god. This quest is in contrast to the will of God, who is a jealous God and desires that we *"Fear the Lord your God, to walk in obedience to him, to love him, to serve the Lord your God with all your heart and with all your soul, and to observe the Lord's commands and decrees"* (Deuteronomy 10:12-14, NIV).

Like the other women, I was deceived when this first came over me. I was ecstatically overwhelmed and could think of nothing else. I found myself telepathically communicating with this unseen spirit until I grew weaker and weaker. At first, I believed this invisible spirit to be the visiting soul of the man who had done this thing to me, but over time, it became more and more apparent that I was infested with demons. I had been mesmerized with the illusion of love, and I had to get free.

Chapter 1

The Beginning

Maybe you wonder how I got here. I have reflected on this many times. I was a different person before everything in my world was turned upside down. I was naïve and hopeful, a girl trying to figure out life who, like most people, went through some difficult times. I had faith in something greater that was guiding my way, but I did not realize the battle against the principalities of darkness was here and now. I was waiting for my true love to come into my life and save me, but somewhere on my path, it all went wrong. It turns out that no man can save your soul. Only Jesus Christ is the way to salvation. I was forced to accept that truth, and once you do, there is no going back. Though I cannot change my past, I can repent and move forward.

After my chakras were opened and I was exposed to being touched by the unseen spiritual world, I went through a period of cognitive dissonance. I could not believe what I was experiencing because it was so unreal, like nothing I had ever known. This experience was part of a reality that I was not prepared for. After working through my anger, confusion, sorrow, guilt, and frustration and praying to God to take it all from my mind, I have come to realize that there are reasons why I should not forget my experiences and the pain. I cannot unknow what I know, and God would not want me to. He takes what others meant for evil against me, and He uses it for good (Genesis 50:20).

Had I not come to know that there is a dark side, I would not have recognized my own sin and been able to repent and be in good standing with God. I made some very regrettable choices along the way, and had I not come to a place of recognition, I might still be making those types of choices to this day. I would not know to question the status quo and fight against the ways of the world to do what I now know is right. Most of us would rather go along to get along because this is the path of least resistance. When we allow ourselves to heal by processing our emotional scars instead of suppressing them, they, like tattoos, can remind us of our history and our growth. What lesson is worth learning if we forget the journey? The journey is the evidence of the answer and the proof of what we have come to know. My personal experience has made the battle between good and evil very real to me, and now I can confidently say that in my heart, I choose good, and I choose God.

My Father

We grew up in the lower-middle class. My father worked as a machinist. He was the only male in his family, and despite being favored by his parents as the only son and being the only one of his siblings to attend college, he struggled to find himself on a path toward success. He earned a bachelor's degree in psychology and dreamed of being an English teacher, but he never made his way into education. There was always something holding him back. His father believed it may have been brain damage from the time he fell off the tailgate of a pickup truck when the driver forgot that my father was back there and picked up speed heading up the hill. According to his father, he was never the same, and his ambition was lost, but he still had ambition. He went to work daily and did what he knew to bring home a modest income. He loved nature and science and enjoyed inventing things using milk jugs, pool noodles, and old skis that he found at the dump to make sleds, chairs, animal feeders, and just about anything else he might need.

My father was considered average—absolutely average, I read in an old personality test that I found locked in a briefcase in our basement a few years after he passed away. He was genuinely jovial and loved sharing conversations with family and passersby alike. He spent his final years writing and singing music at his favorite hangout and testing his songs on his passengers after he transitioned from being a machinist to working as a rideshare driver. He was a family man who was dedicated to his children and wife. If you knew him, you would never guess he had a strained relationship with my mother. They fought and lived in the same house as though they were living apart, but he never left her. He brought her to appointments, and in his final years after she suffered her first stroke, he managed her medications and her bills.

My Mother

My mother gave birth to me when she was between 18 and 19 years old. She was raised in a family that struggled to get by. My mother's father raised a garden, kept chickens, fished, chopped firewood, and was as self-sustaining as possible. My mother once told me that the last time she ever ate rabbit was when she got the piece with the bullet in it. My grandfather proudly held a shotgun at her wedding, with an enormous grin on his face, and you could tell he was just joking. The fact that I was born nine months later confirms my mother's account that I was conceived during my parents' honeymoon at a cabin by the lake, and not before their marriage.

My parents lived in a small apartment in town for a short time. Financially, they struggled and eventually moved in with my father's parents into the home built by my grandfather in the mid-1950s, just before my father was born. This is where my sister, brother, and I were raised. I remember answering phone calls for my grandmother in a language unfamiliar to me; her family had emigrated from Poland. My grandfather passed away when we were very young, and life became difficult for my grandmother after that. She had been excommunicated from the Catholic Church for marrying my grandfather, who was divorced, and felt very isolated even from close family, often relying on alcohol to cope in her final days. To my knowledge, she passed away from complications related to alcoholism.

The Breakdown

I remember the day that everything changed. I was six years old, playing on my bicycle in the front yard. My father called out to my siblings and me from the porch to come inside. Something was very wrong. My mother was in my parents' downstairs bedroom, and there was an uncomfortable excitement. My father told my siblings and me that my mother was very sick. However, it was not just physical illness. My mother had announced that she was God and called our relatives to come to the house to hear her speak. I felt sorrow and shame. While I was outside in the front yard, my older cousin took this as an opportunity to inform me that we were living in his house, claiming his parents had told him so. Hearing it made me feel like a usurper. Suddenly, my family was broken, and we did not belong. I felt my world fall apart. I mourned my mother. Our relationship would never be the same. For what seemed like years, my mother lay in her bed crying, speaking to God, talking to demons, and rising only to cook and wash dishes.

Over time, our house and yard decayed, like in *The Fall of the House of Usher*. The housework was neglected, and the yard work was abandoned. I was humiliated when a neighbor left a note on our front door asking us to clean up the yard because our house was decreasing property values for the homes in our neighborhood.

Despite all this, I felt God was with me. I was reassured of His presence when I dreamed that while I walked with others, I hovered above the ground while they walked on it. In another dream, I battled an evil spirit in a dark cave out in the middle of a stormy sea. The spirit was like wind in the form of a ferocious demon head and chased me round and round the rocks in the center of the cave while I reciprocally chased the demon back around the center of the cave to combat him. I also dreamed that, out in the desert inside a yurt, an unseen authority commanded me to choose a crown. The bones of dead kings and their deteriorated treasures lay in piles spread out in a circle inside the yurt. I selected a filthy, battered, and tarnished crown, brushed it off, and thought, *This could be nice if I cleaned it up*. Now, I wonder if, in my dreams, Satan met me in the desert and tempted me with riches and a dead kingdom.

Over the years, my mother attempted to find a new normal. I have a fond memory of her helping me find a special place in the yard to plant the grass that I had grown from seed at school. She tried several different medications, each with its own devastating side effects. One caused her to lactate and believe that she was pregnant. Others changed her personality completely in a zombified way. My father preferred that my mother not take any of them. My mother was very intelligent and went back to school, earning a certificate as a paralegal and then as a massage therapist. But regardless of what she attempted, she could not find a professional job or even hold a simple job as a cashier. Whenever she was stressed, her paranoia would get the best of her, and her professional relationships would deteriorate when she expressed her sense of rejection through anger.

My mother sought self-help through New Age materials. She listened to stories on cassette about the wild woman archetype and read countless books on spirituality. I remember her calling my sister, brother, and me together one day to sit around the dining room table and watch as she moved a penny with her mind. She said, "Look, it moved a little," but neither my siblings nor I saw it move at all. Through a psychiatrist, my mother became involved with Reiki and began practicing the technique of transferring invisible energies to promote healing.

As a teenager, my mother attuned me to Reiki using symbols that she was led to create and gave me a copy of the symbols that I have long since discarded. For a time, I practiced Reiki, experimenting with its techniques and I even tried it with a college friend who had also been attuned. As an adult, I attempted to heal sick people with Reiki when opportunities presented themselves. I remember when an older man, who appeared to have jaundice because of his pale-yellow skin, collapsed at the store where I was working. I prayed for him and attempted to channel Reiki. He was taken out on a stretcher, and I was not sure what his outcome would be, but not too long after, he found me at the store and thanked me personally for saving his life. I was one of about ten people who had gathered around him, and I wondered if he had really been healed by my prayers or by the Reiki. For some reason, he gave the credit to me.

Childhood

I was ashamed of my family and of my home, and I crawled into an emotional shell that took me years to escape from. In kindergarten, I hid under the tables. I was quiet and obedient. My mother told me that my kindergarten teacher said that whenever she asked the students to clean up, she had to stop me from helping because otherwise, I would clean up all their messes, and they would not learn to clean up anything for themselves. At home, I held on to this idea as a child, refusing to clean up messes that my sister and brother made, and according to my mother, this caused lots of grief because my sister and brother adopted the same policy of cleaning up only after themselves.

Because I was an extraordinarily shy child, I was placed in a readiness class, while my younger sister, who skipped readiness, went straight to first grade, where we were together. We were our own best friends. In elementary school, she was placed in advanced classes, and by fourth grade, I had moved into the advanced reading group too. The school was my escape. I memorized the times table and learned how to calculate percentages sometime between 3rd and 4th grade. My greatest achievement was winning a dinosaur stamp drawing contest in either 2nd or 3rd grade. I was proud when they took my photograph with the other winning students in front of the school, and I was awarded a stamp collection as a prize. My father collected stamps too.

My teachers and classmates recognized my drawing ability, and I built confidence through my emerging talent. I won doodle contests and was incredibly proud of my Oliver the Cat diorama, which I had created around 3rd grade. In middle school, I was proud to be awarded the Ranatra Fusca award for outstanding creativity during an O.M. competition. My sister and I were on an O.M. team with a couple of friends who remained our friends in high school.

First Baptism

Sometime between elementary and middle school, I was baptized in a rather awkward ceremony as an 8-year-old by a relative who brought me down to a pond near my maternal grandparents' home. This relative told me that it was my responsibility to save my family, or they would all go to hell. I was overwhelmed and confused by this burden. I remember thinking that if my family was destined for hell, then I wanted to be with them. I would be bored and lonely with the angels in Heaven, eating grapes, without my family. I challenged God, saying, "If he was real, he needed to put a Bible in my hands." With that, I went on with my life.

At that time, I had little knowledge of God's Word, and did not understand who Jesus was. My mother always told us the church was evil, and she kept us away from it. She used her own family as an example. Her mother was Catholic and kept a small altar outside her bedroom with a rosary and an illustration of Jesus taped to the wall. My mother told me family tales of dark events and ghosts. As a child, the only time I ever visited a church was with my friend from elementary school. I followed her up to the altar and accepted the communion wafer. I had no idea what it was and took it back to the pew. My friend laughed at me when she realized it, and that is when I learned that those were for eating. I now understand that I should not have received communion from a Catholic Church because I was not eligible. Despite the baptism given to me by my relative, I was not immune from demonic attacks, although for most of my life, I did not recognize the attacks for what they were. Even so, I am certain God and the Holy Spirit have been with me throughout my life. I would not have made it this far without them.

Chapter 2

Loss of Innocence

16 Years Old

When I was 16, I spent most of my time with my sister and our best friend. After school, we hung out with him whenever we were not working at the local supermarket. He drove us around in his little Honda Civic, and we always found things to do, like going to the movies and buying snack cakes. He was the first person we knew to have a computer at home. He had a Mac, and I still remember hearing the modem ring as it dialed up and the computer said, "You've got mail." This was a time when everything was exciting, yet we had an innate desire to rebel.

My mother was more difficult to live with when we were teenagers. I am sure she felt the same way about us. We could stay out all day, and she would not complain, but when we were home, even the smallest things would upset her. If we argued with her, we instantly became her "little bitches" or her "little whores." She would scream at the top of her lungs, breathing fire and rage, and this was how she won arguments. The loudest, scariest person always won. These fights happened regularly before school when the stress of dealing with three teenagers battling over the shower was too much. During one of these fights, I took my car and left for school without my sister or brother. My mother had no choice but to drive them in. We were all late, but me by only a few minutes late. When I got to the front office, I was asked by the student helper what day I wanted to serve detention for being late. I said that I did not want to, and she looked over at the secretary and said, "Well, she's usually a good kid." They let me go. Later on, I felt guilty because both my sister and brother had to serve detention.

Getting to school was always challenging, and the reason was not always transportation. My mother would frequently ask us to stay home, whether to avoid driving us in or just because she wanted our company. My sister and brother averaged between 30 and 50 absences every academic year. I averaged somewhere between 15 and 25 absences because I did not want to fall behind in school. All my worth was tied up in my report cards.

The fights at home were emotionally draining. We laughed them off with the crude, sarcastic humor that we had developed. Watching shows like *The Simpsons*, *South Park*, *Married with Children*, and *Roseanne* on television helped us feel just a little more normal. After one of our worst school morning fights with our mother, we went to school feeling a little off but got through the day. After school, we went to our friend's house, and we were horrified when our mother showed up at his house to drop off a box of donuts. The donuts took the place of an apology. She left immediately, and the moment felt icky and awkward.

My mother had a way of making us feel terrible inside. Christmas was one of those times. It seemed like every year an explosive fight broke out, and she would spend the day crying in her room. One year for Christmas, she bought me a heavy, black, wool cape. I had never seen anything like it, except maybe on Ebenezer Scrooge. As a teenager trying to look cute, I was mortified. My mom had tied up so many hopes in that cape that it broke her heart when I felt completely devastated by the fact that this was my gift. She raged and cried in her room, a victim of my disappointment. Everything was our fault.

Christmas was usually pretty small for us. I had a few great Christmases, though, those were the ones when my Dad stepped up to the plate, putting his inventive genius to work. One year when we were all young, he made us dollhouses, slingshots, and a rocking horse. That was the best year ever. Another time, he remembered and got me the one thing that I wanted. I was a teenager, and all I wanted was a gold locket. Maybe I had watched *Little Orphan Annie* that year. I was disappointed after opening all my gifts and not one was a locket. Then my Dad directed me to the top of the tree, and there it was, my locket, around the angel's neck. I still cry when I think about it. It meant so much.

My mom tried. She struggled, but she tried. I know that she loved us because we were her children. There were times when she would tell us how great we were, how perfect. When she felt that she needed to protect us, she did so fiercely. She protected us from her family and tried to protect us from my dad's family, isolating us from almost everyone most of the time. My mom would battle our teachers if she felt it necessary, and I am sure that she would have taken on the world.

My sister and I were angry about our home life. We were angry about the stresses of school. We were furious about the world. I wore an unbuttoned flannel over my political T-shirts, like the one that said "Clinocchio: Will he ever stop lying?" I remember the shirt well. I pierced the elongated nose with a safety pin. I also wore a Salem, MA pentagram T-shirt. When my Greek Orthodox high school math teacher saw it, he pulled me aside to question why I would ever wear the devil's sign. I argued with him and told him this was not the devil's sign. The devil's sign is inverted. Mine was the right way up for Wicca. I had no idea they were the same, but his concern led me to stop wearing the T-shirt and my pentagram necklace. He was like a second father figure at school. He challenged me when I came in with my jacket smelling like my mother's cigarette smoke. I do not know if he ever believed me when I told him that I did not smoke, but I did not, and I do not. That lecture caused me to confront my mother about her smoking, which resulted in more explosive arguments. Smoking was a coping mechanism for her, and when she finished one cigarette, she moved on to another.

We discovered Wicca at the bookstore. We often escaped reality by spending time at the mall, browsing trendy goth clothing stores, and then heading to the bookstore to peruse books and drink fancy coffee. I am not sure exactly how it happened, but the section on occult books piqued our interest, and I brought home a Wicca spellbook or two. Our friend also purchased magic books, but he kept his books in the trunk of his car, knowing that his mother would not approve. When I first opened the small, purple paperback book, I came across a warning that God would punish magic users seven times over. I was not sure how this was relevant to me because I did not intend to harm anyone, and I did the math out:

$$7 \times 0 = 0.$$

Still, I was hesitant to cast a spell without a cause, and it was a while before I found the cause.

At 16, I thought I had found my forever love in a boy who was maybe a year older than I was. He went to a different high school but was friends with some of my friends. He had long hair and something rebellious about him—maybe his trench coat—but he was kind and intelligent. I found him attractive and thought this was love. I lost my innocence to him in more ways than one. He introduced me to Mary Jane. One night, after hanging out with him, I came home to my concerned parents waiting for me at the door. I think my sister tipped them off. They wanted to question me at the dining room table, which raised an alarm. They were generally never interested in anything I was up to, and of course, I was stoned. They asked me to sit down and pushed a bowl of ice cream toward me to gauge my response. They wanted to know whether I had been using drugs, and I was not sure how worried I should be. They may have been concerned, but there were no real consequences from the conversation, and it felt like they were just doing their due diligence by checking in.

I thought my relationship with that boy would last forever until the day I heard from a girl he knew. She worked at a mechanic shop, and he was intrigued. He thought she was so cool. She told me that he asked her out, and my heart broke open in rage. I took all the jewelry he had given me and had my friend drive me to the other all-night restaurant where he used to hang out with his other group of friends. I threw the jewelry down on the pavement outside the restaurant. There was a large garnet-colored Claddagh ring that he picked out for me, an ankh, and other items I do not remember. A friend of his was kind enough to overlook my indiscretion and brought me inside to buy me a coffee, but my heart was still broken despite the kind gesture, and I had no idea how to heal it. When the night was over, I did not know where to turn.

Figure 1 A collage telling a story of fallen angels and the transfer of power through the sun, moon, and witches to destroy man. The Kabbalistic Tree of Life stores power in the spheres, which appear to escape the walking tree as gas. An owl rests on the tree's head. Crystals in the form of a reverse pentagram, a pyramid, and psychedelic mushrooms serve as tools to access the power and presence of this alternate reality. A hand in the foreground indicates that the viewer, maybe myself when I created this, has ordered the destruction of the man, and set dark powers into operation. 1998-1999, Watercolor on paper

I turned to the Wicca spellbook. I decided to personalize a love spell for him to share my pain so he could understand how much he hurt me. I found a private space outside and set up my pentagram with tokens for the spirits of the north, south, east, and west. I had a tiger stuffed animal that he had given me, and I cast my spell with the intention that he would fall deeply in love with me, but I would be disgusted with him, and he would feel the pain. I repeated over and over the intention of no harm to anyone. Figure 1 explains how the magical process operates. I painted the images with watercolor, cut them out, and glued them onto the black poster board. At the time, I had no idea what the images represented. I thought I was creating fun, creative illustrations of things that interested me.

Time passed by, and I forgot all about it. Maybe a year or two later, when I was feeling high on life, I had the urge to call him, and he invited me out. I took him up on his offer and met him at his home. His mother was there and informed me that it was his birthday, and she wanted me to take him out to eat so they could organize a surprise party for him. I took him out, but I felt strongly that I did not want to mislead him and was not interested in pursuing a relationship with him. I felt terrible about declining to celebrate with him at his party, but I left as soon as I had the opportunity. I am not sure what heartbreak I may have caused him, but it was not long before I realized that the spell had been fulfilled. I had used my will in such a way that it overpowered and controlled both him and me without any awareness on my part while the events transpired.

I was filled with curiosity. What is this power that powers witchcraft? Was it my power? Was I special? I was not worrying much about Satan, although thoughts about God's wrath crossed my mind. Thinking back, I realize that the cartoons and movies I watched were inundated with magical themes. *The Wizard of Oz* was a special movie my family watched on television every year, and I loved the wholesome *Bedknobs and Broomsticks*. I thought I understood magic. There was good and bad magic, and as far as I knew, I was practicing the good magic.

After all, I was not digging up coffin nails like I read about in one horrifying, dark magic book. I learned from ghost-hunting shows that I could cast out unclean spirits by smudging my home with sage. Little did I know that using sage in this manner is also a form of witchcraft. When I consider the magical influences that are all around us, I no longer think of them as innocent or wholesome. I believe this pervasive exposure is an attack on our minds designed to separate us from God, who desires that, *"When you enter the land the Lord your God is giving you, do not learn to imitate the detestable ways of the nations there. Let no one be found among you who sacrifices their son or daughter in the fire, who practices divination or sorcery, interprets omens, engages in witchcraft, or casts spells, or who is a medium or spiritist or who consults the dead. Anyone who does these things is detestable to the Lord; because of these same detestable practices the Lord your God will drive out those nations before you"* (Deuteronomy 18:9-12, NIV).

I knew God was real in my life, but I had no understanding of Jesus and was open to demonic deception. I loved nature and identified more and more as a Wiccan, believing that there was magic in the world around me. One crazy evening, a large number of friends and I gathered at our friend's house, intending to cast a snow spell. We were eager for the first snow day of the season. Together, we sat around his kitchen table with our candles, summoning spirits and sprinkling white rice on the table and floor.

After we were finished, we questioned whether we had missed something and went through the ritual again, this time flicking the light switch on and off and playing holiday music. In a matter of days, a huge, unpredicted storm arrived and took out the power. We were without power for two weeks. It was disconcerting to learn that two people lost their lives in the storm. I realized then that there is power in witchcraft and danger, and I shared what we had done with my mother. She told me that God does not like magic, and this time, the words reached me, and I decided I would not attempt casting a spell again.

The Rose

During my junior year, I became friends with a girl who was a year ahead of me in school. She began inviting me to go out with her, and I accepted. My new friend introduced me to a whole new world, filled with clubbing and adventure. She was Catholic, kind, and came from a great family with a beautiful home, but she enjoyed partying. She encouraged me to get my first tattoo. I had to think about it: What could I get that would be meaningful to me and something I could live with for the rest of my life? I sketched out a blue rose, as seen in Figure 2, to be permanently etched onto my shoulder. The tattoo would be concealed enough not to interfere with my job prospects but placed where I could reveal it if I chose to. The blue rose symbolized impossible love—a love that no man was capable of delivering because it simply did not exist. My mother gave me money to pay for the tattoo as a birthday gift for my 18th birthday. I was a little disappointed that the tattoo artist chose to modify the leaves by changing the shading of the lines, but otherwise, I was pleased with my body art. It told my story: I was searching for a love that could not be.

Figure 2 A drawing of a blue rose with light shading. 1998, Pencil and marker

We went on many adventures together, going to concerts, clubbing, shopping, and going to the city. One time, we visited a male relative of hers in a city several states away and spent the night sleeping under blankets on his floor. I mention this because while there, I had an experience I could not explain. I woke up where we were sleeping, with my hips rocking back and forth, completely engaged in sexual intercourse with something or someone that was not there. I had never experienced anything like this and thought it must have been a dream. As pleasurable as it felt, I was embarrassed and stopped as soon as I realized what was happening, hoping that no one had seen me.

Chapter 3

The Escape

College

After I graduated from high school, I escaped from home by moving an hour and a half away to live on campus at college. I was excited to study graphic design but found myself feeling lonely and rejected for most of my first year. My first roommate moved out, and I struggled to find friends. Eventually, I met a few people who seemed to tolerate me. I was on the third floor, and they were on the fifth. One of the girls was very kind, and we got along well. We were both shy. I would go with the group to parties, but I never felt like I truly belonged.

My second year was similar. Although I was in a different dorm, I had a roommate who could not stand me. We had a challenging relationship. She would lock me out of the room to spend time with a boy who had a room next door to us. When she did this, I decided to lie down in his bed. I was making an even exchange for space, but it was a little uncomfortable because he had a roommate. I tried to get along with her and invited her to come out with me. She agreed, but then I heard her screaming about it through our door, so I let her know that it was not mandatory. I must have embarrassed her.

When we were first moving in, her parents tried to get me to hide all of my supplies under my bed. They bought me cinder blocks to lift my bed and make room for all of my things. I thought our room looked great. Her things were all beautiful. I even volunteered to have our room photographed for an upcoming college catalog, but when the photographer arrived, and my roommate was not there to agree, he let me know that he was not interested in photographing my side of the room. That hurt a little, but I finally understood what my roommate was dealing with. My things were not nice, and she had to look at them. My computer was embarrassing—a used, yellowing tower that my father picked up for me from a guy at the computer shop—and my supplies were in an enormous, gray, plastic toolbox.

My roommate eventually dropped out of school for personal reasons, and I had a double single room for the rest of the school year. I made other friends who lived in the same hall, and life became easier when I felt more like I belonged. We moved in together off campus the following year.

I worked bi-weekly, just on weekends, at the wholesale club in my hometown and several days a week at the grocery store in my college town. I enjoyed traveling home because, as much as I resented it, I discovered that my roots were firmly planted there. I needed regular contact with my family to keep my roots watered and to feel like myself. During my third year in college, I left the grocery store and began working at a fast-food restaurant a couple of exits further down the highway. I continued alternating weekends with the wholesale club. The fast-food restaurant was a significant improvement over the college supermarket. I got off earlier—at 9 PM instead of midnight—and still made more money.

My final year in college came with an enormous surprise. After attending a meeting about study abroad opportunities, possibilities opened up for me. I realized I could do this and would earn enough credits for a minor in Spanish. After getting approved for an additional $5,000 loan at the financial aid office, my heart was set on spending my final semester in Seville, Spain. I was so happy thinking about it while driving down the highway. I could never imagine something as wonderful as this happening to me. I thanked God and cried. I felt a bit guilty, too, for leaving my roommate behind. We had planned to move into an on-campus student apartment together, and I never spent a night in it.

Driving down that highway, I reflected on my life and the support I had. I thought about my dad, how much he meant to me, and how much he had done for me. I cried, mourning him as if he had already passed, thinking about how I would lose him one day. I thank God for the opportunity to grieve him because when my father did pass, I was not prepared. He had been in the hospital for weeks, but they were shut down to visitors due to COVID-19, and we could not see him. Even calling him was a challenge because he struggled to see due to several small strokes he had while there. I did not even think he was going to pass away; he was waiting for surgery. At the same time, I was struggling with a personal crisis—a spiritual attack—that kept me distracted from all the little things. I have so many regrets now.

Figure 3 A flamenco dancer in a red dress lifts her dress as she dances to the guitar of a solo guitarist sitting in a chair on the cobblestones of Seville. Two bulls wander beside three large roses resting on the cobblestones at La Feria. 2017-2018, Acrylic on canvas

Spain

My time in Spain was both wonderful and challenging. The pain of being separated from my family while in a strange country reminded me that my roots were still firmly planted at home. I used a calling card to call home about once a week. I felt lonely and disconnected while I was away, but I also met a wonderful woman assigned to me by the school to immerse me in Spanish culture. She showed me around the city and took me on trips across the country. We visited a pastry festival, La Feria, the beach at Matalascañas, and watched flamenco dancers. We also went shopping and out with her friends. Years later, I painted my impression of La Feria, as seen in Figure 3. I felt like an awkward giant among small, beautiful people.

I had a good American friend among the students, too. She was very blonde, and it seemed that wherever we went, we attracted special attention. One afternoon, we were chased down the street and paddled by an older man, something we were told happens to blondes. Another afternoon, while at a fast-food restaurant, a young man came up, kissed me on the cheek, and told me he loved my athletic build. All the girls around me were stunned.

Twice, people attempted to rob me. During our week-long break from classes, I stayed behind in Spain, thinking I could not come up with enough money to travel to Rome with the rest of the students. I decided to bring a novel to the park and sat on a bench to read it. My break lasted only minutes before I saw a man hand his guitar to another man and come over, demanding that I take out my cell phone to call the police. I was aware of this trick to steal phones and declined. I then picked up my things and left the park, with the man walking beside me until we parted ways at an intersection. It was very awkward.

Another time, while my friends and I were walking and eating ice cream, two girls approached us and asked for money to buy some ice cream too. We told them we had none, but as I continued walking, the Euros in my pocket clanged together, and one of the girls reached into my pocket to help herself. I reacted by kicking at her. The other girl raised her books over my head, threatening me before they both fled.

Despite these incidents, we experienced many wonderful things. We saw the UEFA Cup match between the Spanish and Celtic football clubs, and the flood of green and orange stripes throughout the city was impressive. We also witnessed La Semana Santa, La Carnival, the Alhambra in Granada, Roman ruins, and the cathedral in Seville. I was in awe of the cathedral and felt what seemed like spiritual energy emanating from it and even from the cobblestones wherever we traveled. One night, while working on my schoolwork in the living room of my señora, I felt an even more intense energy, as if a thousand spirits were touching me. It was a new and frightening sensation, and afterwards, I tried to avoid it by finishing my work earlier in the evening. I had never felt anything like it at home.

Home Again

I had a boyfriend waiting at home. I met him at the fast-food restaurant where I was working months before I left for Spain, and somehow, I knew that we were meant to be together. When I first met him, I felt an actual spark jolt in my leg when we sat near each other in the small office where he was working as the supervisor. I was impressed with his genuine compassion when he accidentally struck the back of my head while tossing a metal tray holder across the kitchen. I was acting completely out of character when I pursued him, asking him out a couple of times until he finally said yes. The first time, he declined because we worked together. I could not accept this because, after all, this was a temporary, part-time job for both of us. For our first date, he took me to the dog track, and he earned enough money by placing bets to cover our dinner. I was impressed.

After I returned home from Spain, we moved in together. I met his friends and his family, and one of his friends caught my attention with a look of pure love beaming from his eyes. I was confused about what I was feeling. At that point, I was committed to my future husband and knew it would be wrong to consider anyone else, but I had to wonder if this was God-ordained. I seldom saw this friend, except when my husband brought me to his house. I would sit on his dark leather couch, almost melting in bliss, while my husband and he chatted in the garage. I had never experienced anything like this before. I felt a warm, fuzzy love hugging me like a blanket. When we left his house, the sensation would end.

Long after my husband and I moved into my parents' house, I felt his spirit come to visit me. I could not see him, but somehow, I knew it was him. The spirit climbed on top of me while I was lying in bed, and I felt a love greater than any I had ever known. An intense, painful longing took over my heart. The pain was severe, and I prayed to God to take it away. I knew it was wrong to feel love for this man, and I could not surrender myself to him because I had made a commitment to my husband before God. God answered my prayer immediately. The spirit left, but I felt in my soul that we would be connected again in the future. After that, I would only see this man once a year at a family event, and our interactions were friendly. Before leaving to go home, he would tap me somewhere on my shoulder or hand, and I knew that if I focused on the touch, his spirit would connect with me again. I would try my best to avoid thinking about him in the days and nights after our family gathering. It was not until I learned about Kabbalah that I understood what I was experiencing. I can now say that three times, men have tried to connect with me in this way in person and several more times from across the internet.

Within two years, my husband and I were married and had our first child. I thought we were a good match because our differences complemented one another. He was simple, and I was complicated. He liked dogs, football, and beer, and he liked to work. He held two jobs until he began earning enough to live comfortably from one. I had just graduated with my bachelor's degree in graphic design but was quickly discouraged from applying for jobs after two brutal rejections. I was told I could not be hired because I had no experience, and I thought this was absurd because I had spent the last four years studying to work in the field. Then, I was told that I could not be hired because I did not own my own house and I would not fit in. I felt hopeless, and I went back to working in retail and began climbing up the ladder by accepting promotions at one store and then again at another after we moved north. Shortly after my first child turned one and my second was born, I accepted a salaried position as an assistant manager further south. My husband had just been laid off, so we moved.

Chapter 4

Prisoner

South

My schedule was consistent for a time, but then it changed. I was given an alternating schedule, and it was no longer possible for me to consistently pick up my children from daycare. My hours grew longer, and I had to choose between my career and my independence from home. I was not prepared to step down into an hourly position, and my husband could not commit to being home on time from his new job to pick up the children. I chose to keep my job and move my family back in with my parents. There was a daycare center right down the road, and my father could help with transportation.

I was dreaming of owning a home of my own, but that was nearly impossible, especially after staying with my family for a few years. My husband and I took over many of the expenses at my parents' home, and my parents became dependent on us being there. The house was in poor condition, and my mother suffered from mental illness. Duct tape and spray foam were my dad's favorite building materials. Broken windows were never repaired. Screens were full of holes. The floor in the kitchen had rotted under the sink, and the linoleum over it was covered in burn holes. Although my sister helped me paint many of the walls and ceilings before we moved in, the sheetrock walls upstairs were full of holes and covered in ripped wallpaper from our childhood. Yellow from my mother's perpetual smoking bled through the new paint on the kitchen ceiling, even after several coats. The electrical system was outdated, and my husband upgraded the house from a fuse box to a 100 Amp breaker box, but we still had no grounding on the outlets and relied on adapters and extension cords for most of our appliances.

My husband and I paid for many repairs and helped with taxes and utilities. We took over phone and internet bills, put in a new heating and air conditioning system, tiled the downstairs bathroom ourselves, and contributed to groceries. From time to time, when I was overwhelmed with our crowded and less-than-desirable living circumstances, I would research homes for sale, but whenever I mentioned moving, my father shared his disappointment and frustration. He insisted he would not be able to live with my mother and that he would lose the house if we ever moved out. I felt trapped.

As time went on, work became more consuming. My workdays grew longer, often exceeding 12 hours, and sometimes, I would be sent to work at other locations for a week at a time, away from my family. I missed many holidays and weekends with my children, and I was exhausted physically and mentally. I was chasing a dream, hoping for more money to buy a house, but never saving, and I struggled to find time to enjoy life. If I had two or three consecutive days off, I slept for the first, cleaned and went to appointments for the second, and spent the third day regretting that I had to return to work the next day.

I barely noticed when my mother's smoking created a health scare for her. To save money, she switched from buying cigarettes to stuffing cigarette tubes with Native American pipe tobacco. Her lungs were damaged after all those years of chain-smoking, and she struggled to stay awake while sitting at the kitchen table, smoking, and bouncing her leg up and down. She dozed off, burned her arm with a cigarette, and blamed some woman she knew once upon a time for making her do it. I was concerned but did not realize how concerned I should be. I was angrier at her for smoking and burning herself than anything, and this did not seem too out of the ordinary for her. She always lived in a different world. My sister realized something was wrong when she stopped by to visit. My mom was a pale, gray color that I had not even noticed. My mom was brought to the hospital, and we found out that her oxygen level had dropped to 65. The medical professionals said they were surprised that she survived. She went into rehab in 2011 and came out a few months later with an oxygen tank and a CPAP machine. Amazingly, after a stroke sometime around 2019, she stopped needing the oxygen and the CPAP.

Still, through all of this, she was my mother. When I was home, I spent a lot of time chatting with my mother. Her reality overlapped mine, and whenever I was overwhelmed at work, I would bring my troubles to her. She always said that she could speak to God, and I would ask her to pray for me, especially if I thought that I might be in trouble for something that happened at work. I always felt better when she told me that God told her everything was going to be just fine and that I was perfect, a complete perfection.

My mom almost always cooked our meals. We ate lots of vegetables and meat boiled, fried, or broiled in cast iron. She loved cooking shows and would occasionally spoil us with a dessert or something exotic. She told me that God gave her recipes while talking to her in the kitchen. Other than cooking, my mother would wash dishes and occasionally wipe down a surface. She rarely swept. I remember a day when I was home outside in the backyard, and the Mormons stopped by to spread their word. With the window open, I could hear the entire conversation. My mother sat confidently, trying to convince them that their religion was wrong and that she already had a relationship with God. As they left, I overheard them saying, "She doesn't even sweep the floor." I felt so ashamed. I lived there too, but work was draining everything I had out of me.

My mom spoke about her angel husbands regularly. She told my father that she had spiritually divorced him and married her angel husbands instead. She married her first angel husband with a large, princess-cut garnet wedding ring that she bought for herself on a credit card. The number of her husbands grew weekly. She had at least 39, some with names like Shananda and Satan. I could never hear them speaking, but she spent hours each day talking to them and even having audible, orgasmic sex with them. She shocked me when she told me that God pulled out his enormous penis and put it on her stomach, and it was the size of a football. I struggled to believe that our Father in Heaven would engage in those types of activities with his people.

My mother's husbands told her she was a "Big one." She was a baby god growing up, and she often spoke of her "Momma," something I understand to be like Mother Earth. My mom described pulling energy suckers off her momma and saving her from near death. My mom was giving birth to new universes with her angel husbands. These would be places where we would all go to live. She spoke about battles in the "awares," which she described as a spiritual shield around a person that protects them from others and collects information that is received directly by God. Often, my mother would accuse others, like the president, distant family members, and members of my father's family, of coming into her awares and trying to steal her money or, worse, sucking her nipples and physically assaulting her. She would launch spiritual assaults against whoever she accused and posted her accusations to social media, a place that she originally used to connect with family. She claimed to be the real QAnon and took credit for a number of its teachings. She was capable of creating accounts and controversy.

It was obvious that a lot of what my mother was saying was not true, but I struggled with many things. I did not have an understanding of how Heaven and Hell work apart from what my mom told me all my life, and I wondered if she had inside information. After all, she had proven that she had a supernatural "knowing" several times. One time, her sister called her on the phone looking for guidance because something was making her feel very uneasy at home. My aunt lives many states away toward the center of the country, and my mother has never gone to see her, but still, my mom was able to tell her that she felt uneasy because there was a snake in her attic. It turns out there was a snake in her attic.

Long before this, there was a time when my family was visiting her parents at their home, and my mother knew that something was very wrong and we needed to get home right away. When we got home, it turned out that my baby brother, maybe 4 years old at the time, had placed a brown plastic cup upside down over the light bulb of the lamp in his room, which was missing its light shade. The cup was melting down around the bulb and beginning to ignite by the time we arrived home. With unexplained insight like this, my mom was able to pull her family and even a friend or two into her world. She built people up by granting them positions of power and making them feel special.

I was the Queen of North America, and although I never really believed that part of me wondered if it could be true in the spiritual world that she was accessing. As a god, my mom made many rules for her kingdom. She would rule all the nations and had a husband assigned to her from every race. She was the mother of all people. Women could not wear pants. Schools would all end. She would own all the houses around us and move her family into each one, and she would keep chickens in her kitchen and have fresh eggs every day.

Her teachings had an impact on me. I avoided becoming a schoolteacher for many years, in part because I had the idea in the back of my mind that schools would disappear in the future. I was introduced to many conspiracy theories at an early age and believed that there could be something to this. Eventually, I started looking into getting alternative certification to become a teacher. I needed a healthy change that would allow me more time with my family and enable me to work at a place where I felt I could add value. My father had always wanted to be a teacher, and this seemed like the perfect solution to gaining a normal work schedule and being more present for my children.

Sometimes, when I lay down at night, I would look up and see spirits flying around the light fixture in my room. Like ghosts, they were dark, eerie, and mostly transparent, flying round and round. My young son asked me what they were. He saw them, too, in his room, and this was enough for me to begin praying to God that He protect my family from all harm. There was something in our home that was not of God.

The Answer

As I grew increasingly frustrated with work and life, I found myself calling out to God in prayer. I had worked my way up to a promotion as a co-manager at a store just over an hour away from my home. After my long commute and working long nights that stretched into long mornings, I struggled to stay awake while driving home. I recall nearly hitting a neighbor who was driving just a quarter mile down the road from my house. I tried to keep my eyes open, but they were heavy, and I could not keep them open for more than a moment. Loud music had no effect, cold air did not help, and smacking my face did nothing to keep me alert. Had it not been for the neighbors' horn, I would have plowed straight into their car.

God answered my prayer in the form of a dream. In my dream, I was attending college, but for whatever reason, I was already late. I was at the office of the registrar but had no idea what my schedule was, who my professors were, or where my classes were being held, but I knew that my classes had already begun, and I needed to get there. I had this dream three times, and each time, I woke up sweating profusely with panic until relief set in when I realized that I had already finished college and earned my degree. After the third time, I had this dream, I understood that God was talking to me and telling me that I needed to return to school. Before this dream, I was hoping to avoid going back to school by finding a teaching job with alternative certification, but I could not find a school interested in hiring me without proper certification. I had no desire to go back to school and take on more debt.

Now it was time. This was a big step moving forward. It was a challenging step because it meant falling backward. I had avoided returning to school because I did not think I could afford it and because I could not start working in a part-time position without losing a significant amount of my income. My salary was more than I had ever made, and I had bonus potential, too. My identity had become entangled with the idea of being a manager. Stepping down meant a loss of status and taking on shame. For two or three years, I struggled with the possibility before God finally reached me with His message, and I took the leap of faith. My bonus paid for part of my schooling. My husband and loans paid for the rest.

I joined a master's degree program in education and began taking online classes while continuing to work as a salaried manager for the first semester. The online classes were much more demanding than I expected and required lots of reading, long papers, and frequent comments with citations on the online blog. I knew that I had to be honest with my boss and let him know that I intended to step down.

This coincided perfectly with changes at the company. They were eliminating my position, and after a few months, I stepped down into an hourly role at another location with a store manager I already knew. Both my store manager and my new assistant manager showed me a great deal of compassion when I told them as an hourly worker that my goal was to finish school. They valued me for my skills and the knowledge that I had accumulated over the last 11 or 12 years. My supervisor was flexible with my schedule and allowed me to work part-time when I began my student internship.

Not all salaried managers treated me as well. One manager, who had been kind to me before when she worked in a position beneath me, threatened to hold me accountable for insubordination when I questioned the instructions that I was asked to follow during inventory. As she came into the store manager's office and lectured me, I could feel tangible shame as if it were not mine but belonged to others on my behalf. This shame was almost like a separate entity. I confirmed this several years later after I had stopped working for the company and returned to say hello to the store manager. Although, at that point, I had moved on and begun working as a teacher and had no feelings of ill will or regret, the moment that I stepped into my store manager's office, I felt the same shame again. It was not mine, and it stayed behind in the office when I left.

Chapter 5

A New World

Catholic School

Finding a job was challenging. I had a master's degree but no experience other than my internship working in education. I created a resume and applied to many schools, but I wondered whether any public school would be interested in hiring a new teacher for the pay that a master's degree should bring. A Catholic elementary school was the first to offer me a position. I worked two days a week, teaching seven classes. I supplemented my pay by continuing to work at the store part-time for a little longer. I had very little knowledge of the Catholic faith but was required to incorporate religion into my lesson plans. I was very uncomfortable talking about Jesus and religion at that point, but I made very loose connections to God by tying nature into my lessons. The previous teacher had a science degree and had done the same. She left resources for me to use, and I combined those with my own. Nature was easy to use as a subject because *"For in him all things were created: things in heaven and on earth, visible and invisible, whether thrones or powers or rulers or authorities; all things have been created through him and for him,"* (Colossians 1:16, NIV).

I regret an Ancient Egyptian mask project that we did, focusing on the similarities between Ancient Egyptian beliefs and Christianity. I now strongly believe that the civilization was destroyed for its wickedness as a result of the worship of

false gods. I attribute the demonic encounter that I
experienced a few years later to a man who follows Kabbalah,
which was built upon elements from Ancient Egypt,
including Egyptian myths and gods.

Moving On

A couple of months later, I found another teaching job. The second school was willing to work around my schedule. I stopped working at the store and was teaching five days a week. I did this until the end of the school year, and at the end of the year, I was offered a full-time, hybrid position at the second school and accepted it. I worked hard preparing lessons, teaching, and grading work, but I loved it. Everything felt good. I fit in. The staff was kind, I had more time at home, and I was doing something that I was good at and proud of. I did not feel the stigma of working at a store. I was not making a lot of money, and I did not have health benefits because they were too expensive for me, but otherwise, things were great.

Hypnotism

In January of 2020, everything in my world turned upside down. My son asked me about taking blacksmith lessons, inspired by the show *Forged in Fire*. As a Christmas gift, I decided to purchase lessons for him. I went to talk to the owner at a forge shortly before Christmas. The owner was kind and informative. I brought home the folder of paperwork he gave me and returned a few days later to drop off the completed forms and payment. He encouraged me to start my son as soon as possible because "You never know what's going to happen." I thought the pressure was odd, but he seemed like a sincere man. We talked inside his forge until he finally took a seat in his recliner. I took this as a sign that it was time to go. On my way out, another man entered the forge beside me and gave me an unusual glance as if to say, "It is going to be tasty." I dismissed what he seemed to be implying, thinking, I am married.

It was either late December or early January of 2020 when I brought my son to his first lesson. The building was large and filled with forging equipment, tools, and cabinets. The outside was red brick, and the inside was gray. The ceiling was very high and had large windows at the top, many of which were broken. They let in lots of light and air, which diffused the scent of cigars that the owner smoked. In the center of the large room, numerous anvils on blocks occupied the space between two forges. The owner had a small office area beside the forging area, set apart by furniture that formed short walls. Hammers and metalwork adorned the walls by the entrance along with a chalkboard, a recliner, and a table with a coffee pot. Toward the back of the space, there was a doorway to the sink area and a stairway to a hall that connected to a karate studio.

I enjoyed the energy in the place. Everyone seemed to glow. The people at the forge felt like a family. Several were there working as helpers. As my son was being instructed and went back and forth between heating metal and hammering it, I sat by the coffee maker at the table, sketching the shop and the people inside and chatting with some of them. I brought my sketchbook because the ride was about an hour long, and I wanted to keep busy; besides, it was an interesting place. We went for lessons once a week, and all the forging equipment was rearranged after the second or third lesson. I could not complete my sketches, so I gave up working on them entirely. I sat and relaxed and just chatted instead.

The owner highly encouraged me to sign my son up for his karate class to help him develop more balance and coordination. That seemed like a great idea to me, so I spoke to my son and encouraged him to join. He was interested, so the next time we were offered a trial by the owner, we accepted it. The owner began talking about symmetry and balance, and I jumped into the conversation, describing the symmetry and proportion in the human face and body. The owner took this as an opportunity to give me a demonstration of the outer rim theory, a term he used to describe his actions later when I mentioned them to him in a text. He stepped in close to me, standing to my left, and positioned his right elbow in the center of my chest. I was not sure if I should pull away, but I did not. After feeling the resistance of my sports bra, he pushed back further until his elbow was resting firmly against my chest. Then, he pivoted his wrist from his elbow, swinging it back and forth, up, and down, repeating, "Head, groin," over and over. His words were hypnotizing. After he was finished, he commented to my son, "See, that is the heart chakra," and he placed his fingers into my heart chakra, which neither my son nor I could see. I wondered if he realized that we could not see chakras because the comment came so naturally from him.

Shortly after, he walked away, and my son continued to work on forging his chisel. Whatever the owner had done to me, I felt very warm and connected to him. When it was time to go, I felt obligated to say goodbye. He surprised me by asking, "You're leaving?" It was time to go. The lesson was over, and I wondered if he had been thinking about me. Later, I suspected that he had been meditating on me because of how he sat and seemed to be pensively concentrating inwardly and because of the events that transpired after this.

The Night

A few nights later while I lay in bed beside my husband while lucid dreaming, I felt a beautiful breeze flowing up through my body. It moved, twirling in a spiral, and I visualized it in my mind. It was a white swirling mist, and I followed it as it made a stop at my root chakra. The breeze began to arouse me in a very uncomfortable way. This continued throughout the next day. The next morning, as I drove, I realized that I was also feeling an intense loving sensation in my chest and heart. I thought back to that strange moment when I left the blacksmith shop feeling so fond of the owner and how he mentioned my heart chakra. I could feel that I was connected by my heart and my root chakras to something outside of me. I was curious but concerned and visualized a pair of scissors to cut the cord to my heart chakra. This worked, and the sensation was released from my heart. I thought I had some level of control and left the root chakra alone because I wanted to know what this was all about. For the entire day and evening, I walked around uncomfortably overstimulated but trusting that somehow, that night, I would find relief.

That night, as soon as I lay in bed, the process continued. What had been uncomfortable became orgasmic as I felt an explosion in my root chakra. My body jumped up in the bed, and I was surprised that my husband did not wake up. As this happened, I heard the voice of a young man speaking inside me to someone else, saying something along the lines of, "Holy Shit." I was fairly certain the blacksmith was responsible for this, and I began to wonder what he could be doing to me. The breeze continued traveling upward, moving toward my heart. Then I heard another voice say, "This is a mess. We are going to have to clean this up." I knew it meant all of the connections from my heart to other people. By this point, I had so many severed relationships with former boyfriends, and I loved my family and so many people I had worked with. I argued with the voice, using my mind to tell it not to cut my family from my heart. Then I heard nothing. The breeze moved up into my head, trying to guide me toward the crown chakra. I was confused and visualized an Egyptian crown.

Princess

By morning, I was ecstatically in love. An intense love filled my chest, and I was glowing from the inside out. I had no pain. My soul had detached from my body during the explosion, and I was floating inside myself. I lay in bed, with my head resting on a pillow, marveling as white-gloved hands assembled a beautiful crystal crown on my head. It buzzed and tinkled. When I moved, the crown collapsed and then reassembled itself. I smelled lotus flowers as I heard the fragrance puff into the room every few minutes. I was a princess. Was this real?

From the time I was a little girl, I was surrounded by images of princesses and the idea of magic. I related with the princesses of the fairy tales who eventually rode off with their true love to live forever after. I was like the princess from *The Princess and the Pea*, particularly sensitive and a real princess who would pass the test despite my outward appearance. As a child, I spent a lot of time sketching princesses of my own, beautiful, and elegant ladies in gowns. I had been drawing versions of myself, and I wondered why a princess should not look like me. At times, I felt like a princess. Were stories of princesses told to prepare little girls for this? Was this God's plan for me? All my thoughts, all my hopes, my dreams, were they coming true? I was living in a fairy tale.

Chapter 6

Deception

Figure 4 A girl who loves nature is lost in the wilderness. Evil has entered her, and it can be seen in the red irises of her eyes and devilish horns formed from leaves in her hair. The devil tries to capture her in a noose to take her life by tempting her with the promise of impossible love. God cries down on the earth, watering the land and bringing new life. Between 2003 and 2005, Oil on canvas

Angel Husband

My mom had been telling me that I would have an angel husband just like she did. She told me that I would have many, but I would be their only wife because that is how it was. Was this my angel husband? Maybe he was. What I was feeling was magical. When I sat on the couch and put my feet up, they were instantly massaged with vibrations. Despite the cold weather, my feet were no longer chilled but felt warm. I had no hunger and thought I might not even need to eat. My husband commented on how much he enjoyed the change in my demeanor. He described me as more pleasant because I sat silently and contentedly. I could not explain what was happening to me, to him, or anyone. There was no way for them to understand, and I did not have words to describe what I was feeling.

I realized that the spirit was communicating with me. It moved around in my body and stopped in places as if to ask me about them, especially wherever I had a previous injury. I was not sure if this was out of love, concern, or curiosity or if it was trying to heal me. I was sexually aroused nearly 24/7. The spirit rubbed my backside and calf muscle as if to say, "Nice," and at times, it penetrated me from behind while I washed the dishes. It erotically touched the small of my back, causing my back to arch whenever I took a shower. The spirit was with me in the bathroom when I used the toilet and during every other embarrassing moment. It was with me while I was at work with staff and students. It knew all of my thoughts, and I could not get away from it. My only relief came while teaching, when my mind was completely focused on what I was doing and on my students. This was the only time I did not feel the spirit at all. But the moment the class ended and the students were gone, it would return. Cognitive dissonance set in. I was in disbelief about what I was experiencing. It was not real. It could not be real, but I felt it. Sometimes, it would smile on my face. I could feel it pull the left corner of my mouth up high as if to agree or laugh in a mean-spirited way at me. This disturbed me because it felt like a wicked presence was with me. I struggled with the lack of privacy and peace. I was looking forward to the next blacksmith and karate lesson, hoping that I would have some answers.

Every night, when my mind was completely consumed, focusing on the spirit, the experiences grew more intense. Purple flames with dragon eyes burned when I closed my eyes. The spirit acted like a serpent crawling up my chakras and moving around within me. I would ask yes or no questions with a poke to the left for yes or to the right for no, but the serpent would slither from side to side, confusing me unless it wanted to answer. I felt as though every part of me was being explored physically and spiritually, and I wondered why, but I still felt the intense love in my chest and intense vibrations throughout my body. Sometimes, I felt like I was falling, and sometimes I felt like my spirit was ascending. I began reading about chakras to gain an understanding of what and why I was experiencing this.

When the next karate lesson came, I got an answer but not the explanation that I was looking for. As soon as the owner saw me, he wiggled his fingers at me while standing by his desk several feet away. I instantly felt a tickle in the left side of my chest, and he grimaced at me. It was him. The sexual touching stopped only while I was there, but I was still floating, still vibrating, and very confused and feeling in love. I looked at him, wondering what this was. Did he think I was special? Did he love me? I felt strong love in my heart for him, but when I looked at him, no love was there. He was an old man, and I told him so in my mind. I was taken aback when he walked by and made a comment referring to himself as a "young man" in what felt like a hostile way.

Over the next couple of weeks, this continued. I was nearly unable to function at home because I was constantly aroused and could not escape the sensations or the physical pressure caused by the presence in my head. I took lots of naps, trying to find peace or relief, but found none. I thought that if I could just get rid of all this, I could function normally again. Something inside me responded, telling me, "No, to get better, I need to get moving and keep living my life." I spent a lot of time talking to the spirit, thinking it must be an angel husband, and I insisted that we were already married. It was as if I had no control over myself during these conversations because it did not feel like me speaking.

Another time, I asked the spirit to leave, and it briefly did, but instantly, I felt cold, broken, empty, and in intense emotional pain. I asked it to come back in, and it did, making me feel warm, loved, and well. I was sure I must have control over whether it could stay, and I asked it to leave and come back two more times. The final time it left, I felt so broken that I apologized and told the spirit not to listen to me the next time I asked it to leave. It stopped listening to my requests when I told it to get out. I regret this now, but at the time, I had no idea what I was dealing with and was completely overwhelmed. After this, the owner's demeanor seemed to shift from kind to wicked and greedy, as if he had pulled a trick on me and gotten away with something.

The spirit kept me up at all hours, exhausting me and assaulting me. I could feel demons clawing and climbing under my skin. There was an echo chamber in my mind where all my thoughts echoed as if in a cavern. I felt eyeglasses being assembled on my face, with lenses clicking back and forth, changing my vision with each click. I felt cones being attached to my ears. A pressure moved around in my head, causing migraines and I felt an uncomfortable energy pull from my stomach, reminiscent of the sensation I felt when pregnant, making me feel ill. The spirit seemed to move around in my face and body, and I was concerned I might be exposing children to this evil. Still, I felt intense love in my chest. At times, my heart burned with love as if it wanted to consume me. It hurt so much that I cried. I broke my ankle, frantically trying to run away from it in my backyard, teary-eyed and stumbling. The spirit numbed my ankle, and I walked on it anyway, ignoring the swelling. Was this man trying to help me grow spiritually? Was this love? I was now having serious doubts and needed to know. The love felt real, but the torment was extreme.

I continued bringing my son to lessons, hoping for answers. As soon as our car was getting close to the building, the sensations I felt grew intensely. After we arrived, my son worked at the forge, and I chatted with others who were there while pretending to be fine. I was yearning for touch, but each touch resulted in a spiritual attack. These attacks happened on several occasions. Even though I felt as if I was in love, I was suspicious and frustrated. I thought to the owner, *I have lots of secrets, and I am not going to tell you any of them,* and he walked by me, stopping just long enough to poke me three times in the neck. That evening, every secret I ever had slipped out from hiding and exposed itself in my thoughts.

Another time, the blacksmith touched my shoulder, and the spot where he touched me became like an entryway that allowed spirits to travel freely inside and outside of me. On another occasion, he attached a single wing to the small of my back, causing me to gently sway in circles for days until a spirit burned it off. I wore that wing to a professional development conference with my colleagues, gently swaying and experiencing a form of déjà vu. While I was there, events from a dream transpired. I found myself scooping a pile of jello onto my plate in the cafeteria, later discovering that I had mistaken jelly for jello. It was an embarrassing moment that I had already experienced several weeks earlier in my sleep. The synchronicities did not end there. While I was driving with my daughter to visit my old college to attend a theatre production, I shared memories of my first dorm. When I returned to school where I taught, one of my students shared a dream she had about me. She repeated everything I had told my daughter about my dorm days before.

While I was at the forge, I was looking for clues and wondered about the other people there. One day, it seemed everyone had been given a special job to help the owner clean the shop, except for me. I noticed one woman moving heavy objects from a drawer. I asked her if she needed my help, and she said, "No, I would do anything for [him]." I thought this was strange. Maybe he had done to her what he had done to me, and she was in love with him. But after that day, I never saw her again. That day, I wanted to be included by helping with a job and was very upset to be excluded. I was very angry that the owner kept walking by me and ignoring me, and I felt a burst of rage come from me directed at him. He felt it and nearly fell over but then came over to sit quietly by me and allow me to speak. I asked him for a job to do. He thought about it for a while and took me back to the kitchen to wipe down an old metal case. I wiped it, but none of the discoloration came off. Then he gave me another job. He brought over his welding helmet, and I used paper towels and water to remove all the dust. It took many wet paper towels, but I stepped aside from the sink and waited to finish while a woman, who I presumed to be his wife, washed her vegetables. I wondered about her. Did she know he did this to me and the others? Would she be angry? Was she a witch? Later, he told me she was his girlfriend. He complimented the job I did cleaning the helmet, and I was happy to have helped.

Chalkboard

I continued to seek out answers and made mental notes about my surroundings, like the strange equations on the chalkboard. A square fits in a round hole. Volume equals love. Is this how much spirit or soul he was filling my heart with? I asked my mother if she understood any of this. She identified the square peg fitting into the round hole. I was still unsure if this man was a guru who wanted to help me ascend spiritually or an angel husband. He would not volunteer any information, so I would ask him questions telepathically. "Do you have children?" He told me that he had a daughter. This was half-truth because I later learned that he had a son. "What can I eat?" He offered me a type of fermented seed or nut, which I declined because I was not sure I could trust him at this point. I still had no sensation of hunger, but I would eat meals anyway because, as a teenager, I had attempted a starvation diet and knew that not eating would make me very unwell.

Black Wedding

When I was at home, I was still overwhelmed with physical sensations all of the time. I felt intense love in my heart chakra but was growing increasingly frustrated with the pain and arousal. I was filled with lust beyond control, and it could not be satisfied. It was driving me mad. I repent for the inappropriate thoughts I had in those days. I started to demand answers. I wanted to know if there was a purpose behind all of this. Was there an intention for some type of relationship? Friendship? Romantic? If nothing were to come of this, I could not allow this connection to go on any longer. I needed a resolution or closure so I could find peace again. The spirit allowed me no peace. Often, I would not be able to sleep, and if I did fall asleep, I would wake up at 3 AM to something poking me in the leg, arm, or shoulder.

As I demanded answers, the spirit indicated inside me that we would be married and live together. This made no sense to my rational mind, and I was not sure how this could be possible, but I wanted to know. I continued working as usual and was planning an end-of-the-year event for the school when the spirit tried to remind me that I would be leaving the school and did not need to work on anything. Of course, I was going to continue planning and completing my obligations.

I brought my son to the next karate lesson as usual, having no idea what to expect. When we walked up toward the entrance, I noticed the owner's truck was running, and the rear driver's side door was left wide open. I felt something in me was telling me to climb in. I was terrified, and the pit of my stomach screamed to me that entering that truck would mean my death. My son and I passed by the truck and walked up the stairs and into the karate studio. I sat down in the waiting area and watched as the lesson began. The owner usually instructed the students but was not teaching the class this time.

Moments later, he came in from the entrance by me, all dressed in black in a button shirt with nice pants, and he was wearing cologne. He made an excuse for why he was all dressed up, and I spoke to him telepathically, explaining that I could not enter his truck because I was scared and felt fear in my gut. He asked me about it telepathically, and I realized that the fear was coming from my uterus. I now believe the Holy Spirit was warning me. The blacksmith moved over to sit on a bench directly behind the students, and I studied the ceremonial-looking blades in the case beside me, wondering if they were used on people. I had a strong sense that he would have used one on me if I had stepped into his truck.

While I was contemplating, I noticed another woman walk over to him and whisper in his ear. She came back with a cup of coffee for him before sitting down again. He wiggled his fingers at her, and she reacted just as I had. He had done this to her, too! He left, changed into his karate uniform, and took over teaching the class. Previously, I listened intently to his messages, trying to gain spiritual insight. This time, I chose to tune him out completely and played with a young puppy that was brought in by another mother who was sitting beside me in the waiting area.

At the end of class, the owner approached me and asked if I had listened to his message about forgiveness. *Not really*, I thought resentfully. As the other woman passed by, she was excited when she saw the puppy in my lap, but then she and I exchanged glares. I was furious. Why was he doing this to me and others, too? What was all this? I was hopeful she was not going to be at the blacksmith class afterwards with her boys. She was not, and I was relieved.

When the blacksmith class started, I stood awkwardly near the owner as he sat. I made him uncomfortable by staying just out of sight behind his left side. I was trying to figure all of this out and did not want to be ignored any longer. He turned and looked at me, then told me that all women should be like her. She got him coffee. I was beyond furious. He was insulting me. As a guest, how should I even know to get him coffee in his studio? Why did he do this to me if he did not like me? I left intending to never come back.

On the way to the car, the puppy came running after me in the parking lot. I stopped to scoop him up so he would not be injured and returned him. I was relieved when my son and I finally made it to my car, still breathing. What would he have done with my son if he had done something to me? As we started to pull away, my son turned on the radio, and the song "Jealousy" began playing. I was sure the owner sent it over the radio. There was a day before this, while I was at school preparing a lesson when I knew that the spirit had interfered with my preparation by causing my computer to glitch. My computer was temporarily disabled as numbers began running across my screen. I was now certain that what felt like a fairytale was most certainly a demonic attack. I was angry and sad. My son was losing what had been intended to be a wonderful gift and opportunity for him, and I had a battle for my life ahead of me.

As soon as I got home, I tried to demand answers telepathically. The blacksmith told me that he would have many wives. I cried because I was so upset. I could not understand why I was going through this. How could this man hate me enough to do this to me or anyone else? This was not love; it was cruel. I went to see my mother because she knew how angel husbands were supposed to be. She confirmed what she had told me before: my angel husband would have only one wife, and she told me that this man was not a real angel husband. I told the spirit to get out, but it would not listen. I was not sure how to end all of this. We had never spoken in person about any of this the way we had telepathically. What if he called me crazy? I texted him to tell him that my son and I were finished taking lessons with him for personal reasons. The blacksmith texted me back, asking if I was mad at him. What a strange question if none of this was real. Why would he assume fault? I could not explain my thoughts to him properly in writing.

Shortly after the text exchange, a strong wind, filled with the fragrance of lotus flowers, blew fiercely in my head like a raging hurricane. I poured a glass of water and sipped it, tasting nothing but lotus flowers. I knew I was under an intense attack and went to rest on the couch, waiting for it all to end. The scent of lotus flowers morphed into the smell of beer. I told the owner telepathically what my mom had said and described her as someone spiritual who knows. A few days later, my mom told me that a new man, whom she had not met before, was asking her in the spirit if she wanted to be his wife because he had a few wife positions still open. Wife positions? Now, he was coming after my mother, too. She complained because the spirit orgasmed her heart and penetrated her the way it had done to me.

It hit me—the realization that the blacksmith wanted to marry my ghost. I was standing by the sink in my kitchen washing dishes when I saw a vision of my soul, dressed as a wedding bride, laying horizontally as if in a casket with my arms crossed over my chest, rising above the sink. So many songs seemed to tell this story. In "Black Wedding," the band In This Moment describes a black wedding to an unholy ghost who used to be an angel. Did he marry her ghost? "Fields of Gold" by Sting seems to describe forgetting Jesus, our jealous God while making love in a field. Might this signify turning our back on our God while a woman loses her life for this unjust cause, her body lifted by these unseen forces? As I listened to "The End of the Innocence" play over the radio, I wondered if the song described taking a young woman's life. Nearly every one of my favorite songs took on a new, terrifying meaning for me.

Chapter 7

The Truth

Disclosure

It was time to come clean to my family, so I told them about what I had experienced. My husband began researching sexual disorders to label my condition and decided that I had Persistent Genital Arousal Disorder. The rest of my family labeled me schizophrenic, and it was heartbreaking. I was devastated. My children felt like they had lost their mother. This must have been what it felt like for my mom when people began labeling her as mentally ill. What she felt was so real to her, and she had experienced spirits in the same way I had. I began to realize that my mom's angel husbands were fallen angels. They were demons from Satan's kingdom. Everything made so much sense. My mother had described her angel husbands as recently freed from their chains. All this time, Satan had been deceiving my mother. His demons convinced her that they were angels and that she was a god. She believed that she had given birth to new universes. The concept of using the sexual energy of the Sephiroth to create a microcosm is Kabbalistic. My mother was not crazy; she was under demonic attack.

Figure 5 A princess tries to escape from the peacock in a world she cannot see. She searches to enter the gateway of Heaven to escape the mystical world. Between 2018 and 2020, Acrylic on canvas digitally enhanced

Crown, Tale of Three Sisters

I wanted nothing else to do with this, but I was still wearing an invisible crown. I panicked. What was this? There was a moment at the blacksmith shop when I began to suspect that the crystalline buzzing of the crown was demonic. I started reading frantically, trying to connect the crown to death and came across a tale of three sisters. Two sisters gave the third sister a crown to distract her so she could be killed. The crown was like a prison for her. Was I being distracted? I wanted the crown gone. With my will, the crystal crown disappeared, but the strong buzzing sound remained. Changes in the tone, volume, and frequency of the buzzing sound were more apparent without the masking of the crystal crown. The crown was an illusion. The love that I felt was an illusion. The fragrance of lotus flowers was an illusion. None of this was real, but yet, I felt it. I wanted every illusion gone, and soon, my mission would become to, *"Demolish arguments and every pretension that sets itself up against the knowledge of God, and [to] take captive every thought to make it obedient to Christ."* (2 Corinthians 10:5, NIV).

Searching for Protection

In February of 2020, I began searching for anything and everything that would cleanse me of these spirits. I desperately scrolled through the blacksmith's social media, trying to understand how this had been done to me and how I could end it. I found some clues. *The Zohar* was listed under his favorite books, and it sounded like some type of magic book. I ordered *The Zohar* and every other book on his list and more, after learning that *The Zohar* was connected to Kabbalah.

I also found images and references related to mental alchemy. One photo showed a painting of a diamond bleeding its brains out on a wall in a room with a table beside it, which appeared to have a clear plastic bag filled with different types of women's hair. I might have been mistaken, but I was alarmed. Was the diamond representative of murdered women? In another image, I saw a painting of the Eye of Providence on a small pyramid, with a tear rolling down its face, seemingly because it was not producing energy like the larger pyramids in the image, which were sending out beams of light. Was this the Illuminati pyramid? How was it used? What was all of this?

I ordered books on Tantra, Quabala, Kabbalah, spiritual growth, and psychic protection. From these books, I sought connections that might help me find protection from the spirits that were touching me. I ordered and, for a time, wore clothing designed to block electromagnetic radiation. I purchased crystals to wear and use in conjunction with meditations I found in the psychic protection books. I tried meditating with crystals and buried railroad spikes around the perimeter of my home to generate fields of protection. I saw the use of railroad spikes suggested when searching online for protective objects. I explored the expansion of my energy body, attempting to build shields that would prevent the touching and sexual assaults of the spirits. I attempted chakra meditations that I came across through reading. I tried to raise my vibration to escape all of this and raised it high enough that I could smell the illusion of the flesh of my hands burning. I visualized a Merkaba and began its rotation, trying to ascend out of all of this. I even tried to remove my chakras completely and sought specialists who assist in this process.

Sometimes, the spirit would choke my throat chakra as if to punish me, and I would visualize my chakra being healed to repair it. This happened when I found myself counting boxes of cereal at the supermarket, counting trees along the road while driving, and when I called out profanities at the man. I was trying to distract myself from the oppression, but apparently, this was highly annoying to the man or the spirit. *How rude*, I thought. This man had invaded my mind, where my thoughts were processed, and was punishing me for thinking. It was not my intention to think of him day and night, but my mind was pulled toward him supernaturally. At night, the spirit would burn my toes, and real blisters formed. When I sang in the kitchen, trying to find ways to enjoy my time, the spirit would vibrate my throat to disrupt my singing, but it was only successful on low notes.

I listened to Sanskrit chants to dispel evil. I recited mantras and decorated a paper bracelet with written mantras and floral illustrations, wearing it daily, hoping that positive affirmations would help. To be honest, up until this point, I had always considered positive affirmations something to make fun of. I made a crown of black tourmaline and copper wire, wrapping my hair around it to make it less obvious so I could wear it out during the day. At night, I tried wearing a Santa hat lined with black tourmalines taped inside, and I wore tourmalines in a sock as a pad of protection in my underwear.

The hat worked the first night, seemingly blocking the spirits from moving in my body. On the second night, my husband and I listened as the spirit caused hairline fractures to form in the crystals, and they lost any protective quality. None of these attempts were truly effective. I purchased uncrossing incense and followed the instructions, burning it in little pyramids. I found some relief when the spirits that had been clawing at me, while crawling between my soul and my skin, finally left. However, other spirits were more stubborn. I lit a candle and tried to cast the other spirits out, but I accidentally lit a fire so enormous that it nearly reached the ceiling in the kitchen over my oven where I had placed the candle. Flames shot four feet up.

My mind stopped working as panic set in, and I screamed for my mom, who told me to smother the fire. The lids of our pans were on a wire rack above the stove, and I reached up to grab one to smother the fire, but the heat and flames were too intense. The lids fell, and the candle flew across the room, sending shattered glass and hot wax everywhere. The flames and hot glass burned holes in the vinyl floor wherever they landed. Several fingers on my right hand were burned, and I was in extreme pain. I kept my hand in a glass of water for over an hour, and while doing so, I used my other hand to scrub the wax off the cabinet walls. Every time I pulled my hand out of the water, the pain was unbearable. My sister brought me burn creams, and they helped a tremendous amount. That evening, it felt as though the spirit was healing my hands. The pain left, and over a short time, my hands healed with barely a scar. This experience felt evil, and yet I was still struggling internally with the sensation of love. Why was it healing me? To deceive me?

It was time to end this. I was very weak. My body was shaking. The spirits increased their assaults, and I had no rest except for brief moments when I was completely distracted because I was teaching. Recognizing the witchcraft in what I was experiencing, I asked my sister to take me to a lightworker for help. When I arrived at the counter at the front of her shop, I explained my story and was invited to the back for a cleansing. The lightworker could sense that my energy extended outside of my body. I had intentionally done this through meditation to create a barrier that would block spirits from accessing my chakras. She advised me to keep my energy close to myself for protection. She was able to visualize an energetic metal rod that had been shoved into my skull by the blacksmith, and she pulled it out. Using her singing bowl, crystal wands, incense, and prayers to St. Michael for a shield of protection, she tried to set me free.

As she battled the spirit, it attacked her, crawling on her head. She swatted it away as it buzzed around, and the struggle continued until everything finally seemed still. After hearing my story about love, the lightworker asked if I had considered inviting the owner of the blacksmith shop out for coffee to discuss it. She suggested that maybe it was just love. The suggestion seemed ridiculous to me—it was clearly not love, even though I could still feel the illusion of it filling my chest.

Still, after our session, she gave me a ritual to perform at the next full moon. The lightworker felt it was crucial that I bind this man to prevent him from harming others. She instructed me to create an effigy of him from a sock. During the full moon, I was to bind it with the words she provided, burn it, and then bury it along with all the objects my son and I had received from him. I was also instructed to destroy any remaining evidence of him to eliminate his energy and prevent it from having power over me. On my way out of the shop, I purchased more protective crystals. Although I felt lighter and more hopeful, I knew the spirit was still hiding in my heart—I could sense its presence.

After I got home, all the sensations returned. I continued searching for answers by delving into Kabbalah—watching video after video, reading book after book, article after article, and grimoire after grimoire. Slowly, I found myself able to read between the lines of the metaphorical texts. Although the true meanings are traditionally taught orally, supposedly to men over 40, I was able to decipher them by applying my personal experience and the metaphorical connections I had discovered. I saw myself as the dove undergoing alchemical transmutation through the "Great Work" of the blacksmith, with my heart about to be ripped from my chest as he took my life to transform himself into a king, similar to what happened to the dove in *The Chymical Wedding of Christian Rosenkreutz*.

Death

One night, as I lay in bed, I felt an intense sensation in my head, on the back, right side of my skull, as though it had been pierced by a sharp object. The sensation was so vivid that it felt like the object had penetrated through bone. The pain was overwhelming, and I was filled with fear. Would this be the end for me? My thoughts turned to my children and my husband, *What would they do without me?* When my daughter came in to say goodnight, I worried it might be the last time I saw her. I managed to say goodnight but fought to hide my fear from my husband and children.

I felt an unusual sensation in my nose, as though liquid was pooling and dripping beneath the surface of my skin. It was as if I was losing a significant amount of blood. Over the next few hours, I felt my body gradually shut down, with my arms growing numb. An unseen presence seemed to jump onto the bed beside me, giving me a gentle shove as if to assess my condition. I lay there, wondering about the fate of my soul, while I listened to my husband's rhythmic breathing and found a deeper appreciation for life.

Eventually, the sun began to rise, and I realized that I had survived until morning. Slowly, I attempted to wiggle my fingers and was relieved to find them in working order. Everything was functioning normally. All of this must have been a product of the blacksmith's imagination. Satan can do nothing without the consent of God.

On several more occasions, I experienced what seemed like the blacksmith's imagination. Another night, I found myself blasting off in a cartoon rocket ship. I felt the rapid acceleration and grew concerned that he was trying to force my soul out of my body. I let go of the thought, and the experience ended. Sometimes, we played. I attempted to send him mental images, and I received his visions in return. His images were filthy. I tried to move my energy into his body to see if I could gain more insight, maybe from his mind or his sight. Through visualization, I felt as though I was in him but without sight or access to his thoughts.

At one point, I visualized the woman from the karate studio standing with her children on a floor inside an energy building. The building was entirely blue and made up of thick, flat layers as if it were part of a 3D model. There were holes where windows and doors should be. I wanted this woman out of my mind, so I gave her a shove, and she and her children fell to the floor below. This upset the spirit. It immediately gave me a strong message—"No"—by poking me in the right side of my chest. I was frustrated. I was not trying to harm the woman; I just wanted to push her out of my mind. Genuine harm can come from these meditations. I could not think of any other reason why the spirit would be so adamant.

I spent a significant amount of time telling the spirit to leave and explaining my case for why it should go because I had been deceived and had not agreed to the terms of this relationship. After reading a book about the legalities of Heaven, I also tried to explain my case to God, arguing that this spirit should leave because I was wronged. I went about it in an unholy way. I lit a candle and read a three-page script I wrote that justified all of my actions. I was not focused on true repentance, and I did not plead the blood of Jesus. I have since learned that the only justification for our sins is the blood of Jesus. No other evidence will set us free.

Chapter 8

The Darkness of
Magic And
Meditation

Figure 6 A betta fish contemplates the origins of time. Beside him rest 7 spheres. Unknown time frame, Watercolor on paper

Discovery

In my research, I encountered the Tree of Life map and its counterparts, such as the Sephirothic System of Ten Divine Names. In both, ten numbered circles represent the ten Sephiroth, and twenty-two paths connect the circles. By adding the number ten to the number twenty-two, one can say there are thirty-two paths of wisdom, potentially referenced by the thirty-second degree of Freemasonry. The embedded letters and numbers have been compared to keys contained within a secret system that can unlock the mysteries of creation.

This map can be divided into three pillars or channels: the left, center, and right. All Sephiroth are thought to have both masculine and feminine roles, depending on whether they are givers or receivers of God's light. The Sephiroth on the right side of the map are often described as masculine, while the Sephiroth on the left side are considered feminine. This is because the Sephira on the right side directs light to the Sephira on the left side, which becomes the receiver. The light then travels at a diagonal angle to the right, passing through a central Sephira to reach the Sephira on the right side of the next row below. This light or energy is first received by Keter, the top Sephira, also thought to be the superconscious and the Crown or head of the body. It is then sent down to the conscious intellect, or torso, to Chokmah, described as Wisdom, and then to Binah, described as

Understanding. The light then continues diagonally down to the right through Daath called Knowledge, which cannot appear simultaneously with Keter, and into the conscious emotions and the right arm or the Sephira known as Chesed, also called Loving-kindness. The light then flows to Gevurah, the left arm, called Discipline, and downward through Tiphareth, known as Beautiful-harmony, into the right leg, called Netzach or Victory. The light then flows to the left leg, called Hod or Splendor, and then down diagonally through Yesod, called Foundation. Finally, the light travels down to Malkuth, also called Kingdom, or the Shekhinah, or feet, which connects the light energy of God to man. Shekhinah is sometimes likened to the Holy Spirit of the Christian Trinity and is also referred to as God's bride.

This path, shaped like a lightning bolt, is called the Path of the Flaming Sword. I wondered what this map could be hiding and how its mysteries could be accessed, and I sought to learn more. I joined several online groups dedicated to Kabbalah, hoping to gain insight into its secrets and to learn how to end what I was certain was a demonic connection. However, the heavy moderation left me feeling blocked and isolated with more unanswered questions. Where were the people like me—not practitioners, but those who I believed might also be suffering as a result of this practice?

I sought validation by attempting to share the art I was creating to express my understanding and emotions about my experiences, but even my art could not get past the moderators of certain groups. In a group that did permit my artwork, one man suggested that I create tarot cards. I had used chalk pastels to create a woman in a gown standing on a path between the Sephiroth, guarded from escape by a flaming lion. I entertained the idea for a short time but later came to understand that tarot is displeasing to God. I used tarot cards with my mother and sister as a teenager before being convicted by the Holy Spirit. Since then, I have come to believe that the twenty-two arcana of the tarot are associated with the twenty-two paths of the Tree of Life and that the tarot, like magic, draws from the Tree of Life.

In my research, I encountered Kabbalistic grimoires that claim to provide guidance for achieving an intimate relationship or union with God. Many sources describe this as sexual intimacy or an ecstatic or mystical union. I imagined this to be what I was experiencing. How was I being used in this way? What would it mean for my future? I discovered *The Kabbalah of the Golden Dawn*, a system of ritual magic used in Kabbalah to gain access to spiritual forces and esoteric knowledge. I came across suggested guidance for self-purification by living an isolated, nature-oriented lifestyle and the use of ceremonial objects and rituals to assist those following this path. I read about hierarchies, where one must follow specific protocols when attempting to connect with spiritual entities to gain spiritual powers such as invisibility. I came across a spell that referred to two brains and wondered if this might be how I was telepathically communicating with the blacksmith.

I also came across a collection of five books known as *The Lesser Key of Solomon*, which some believe to be evil, filled with black magic, and derived from the practices of King Solomon from the Bible. Some sources suggest that Solomon used sorcery, practiced summoning demons, was a Kabbalist himself, and that "Song of Songs," a collection of love poems in the Bible ascribed to Solomon, is a Kabbalistic text. According to *The Key of Solomon the King*, a separate book containing detailed prayers and rituals supposedly used by Solomon, the use of prayer, pentacles, and perfumes is sufficient for Qabalistic magic. Rituals are practiced with careful consideration of the month, cardinal directions, and symbolism. It is suggested that pentacles are meant to provide protection for the user while also being used to invoke and terrorize spirits into submission. If it is true that Solomon was engaged in magical practices, it means he turned away from God, who detests the use of magic. Could the pursuit of knowledge have led to wickedness for Solomon, just as the temptation to eat from the Tree of Knowledge led Eve to disobey God?

On an online blog, I encountered a post by a self-identified witch expressing frustration about the lack of respect from her clients for the "gods" summoned to perform what the clients referred to as "pussy magic." It seemed probable to me that these Kundalini "gods," or possibly fallen angels or demons, had been summoned to work on me. This would explain the perfection and intricacy of the work done by the white-gloved hands as they assembled individual crystals into the illusory crown that had formed on my head. I felt that no man could achieve this level of precision. The idea of demons being summoned to work on me terrified me, especially because God warns us in the Bible, *"You shall have no other gods before me"* (Exodus 20:3, NIV).

I came across this witch's comments while searching for connections to Kabbalah because she responded to another woman's concern about why women are not permitted to study Kabbalah despite its significance in Jewish tradition. I replied to the second woman with a question about why women would seek to learn about ritual magic used against women anyway, and only moments later, I felt the witch reach out and touch my arms to sense my energy. I wondered if she suspected that I was an oath breaker revealing inside secrets, but I hoped she would understand that I was a victim of this situation and that I was alive because God is real and far more powerful than any demon. God warns us against making oaths (Matthew 5:34-37). I suspect Satan uses oaths to imprison God's people. When they take an oath, they become bound to works that are not of God, and many oaths incorporate curses to bind those who later speak against them. We are blessed because if we confess, Jesus will forgive us, and in the name of Jesus, these curses are broken.

Before completing my teaching certificate program, I created a screen print of fish staring up at an ankh-shaped anchor as seen in Figure 7. I titled it "Contemplation" without any knowledge of the contemplative practices performed by students of Kabbalah or its association with the ankh. At the base of the anchor is a seastar in the form of the inverted pentacle, which is associated with Satan but can also represent the descent of spirit into matter. To the left is a mollusk that can produce pearls, which are reminiscent of the light and spherical shape of the Sephiroth. In "Late December," the band Counting Crows describes oysters without pearls and light attached to a girl. Could there be a connection to Kabbalah?

Figure 7 Two fish contemplate the presence of an ankh-shaped anchor in their home. A mollusk and sea star rest on the sand beside the anchor. Between 2016 and 2017, Screenprint on paper digitally enhanced

Traditions

I found comparisons between the philosophies of Kabbalah, Gnosticism, Hermeticism, and Rosicrucianism, all of which reference esoteric knowledge of God and the pursuit of enlightenment or a mystical connection to the divine. I also encountered literature suggesting that there are connections between Kabbalah and various religions and secret societies, such as Shamanism, Mormonism, Hinduism, Buddhism, and organizations like the Freemasons. It seems that people are practicing various forms of Kabbalah all over the world, and religious affiliation does not appear to be a barrier.

"Enter through the narrow gate. For wide is the gate, and broad is the road that leads to destruction, and many enter through it. But small is the gate and narrow the road that leads to life, and only a few find it" (Matthew 7:13-14, NIV). Many Kabbalists claim they are seeking eternal life and believe that they have uncovered the mystery to obtain it for themselves. However, would God ask his people to violate His Word, which is his will, to achieve eternal life? God's will is that *"For God so loved the world that he gave his one and only Son, that whoever believes in him shall not perish but have eternal life"* (John 3:16, NIV).

The only references to Jesus that I encountered in Kabbalah suggested that he himself may have been a Kabbalist. One morning, a female voice I suspected to be from a witch sent by the blacksmith, a practitioner of Kabbalah, woke me, saying, "You hate him and his son." It seems to me that Kabbalistic works are in direct conflict with faith in Jesus Christ. Kabbalists seek hidden knowledge through magical practices to gain direct access to the divine without going through the Son.

Gnosticism, Hermeticism, and Kabbalah focus on divine emanations of light that flow from the godhead and form the spheres called Sephiroth, just as depicted in the Tree of Life map. The spheres are considered aspects of God's essence that infinitely pour out and contain the spiritual laws that govern creation. The triad of the Sephiroth —Kether, Chokma, and Binah—forms a Trinity thought by some Kabbalists to be comparable to the Christian Trinity, but I believe this to be Satan's counterfeit version.

In the study of Kabbalah, it is believed that the Sephiroth are connected through four worlds: Atziluth, where the infinite is united with its source; Beri'ah, a world of formless creation; Yetzirah, a world where beings form; and Assiah, where the divine is concealed within a completed creation. Kabbalists believe that by influencing the higher spiritual worlds through prayer and study, they can manifest their will in the physical world that we know.

According to Scripture, *"Not everyone who says to [Jesus], 'Lord, Lord,' will enter the kingdom of heaven, but only the one who does the will of [his] Father who is in heaven"* (Matthew 7:21, NIV).

The intention behind Kabbalah seems to be to manifest one's own will and achieve a divine-like state through the creation of a personal microcosm, rather than living according to the Will of God. Just as Satan tempted Jesus to practice Kabbalah by promising hidden wisdom and power. The ultimate goal for a Kabbalist is to become like a god and the ruler of his or her own universe or microcosm, gaining complete creative power using the sexual energy obtained through the Sephiroth.

It crossed my mind that the ten Sephiroth may represent the ten-horned beast described in Revelation in the Bible because much of the practice of Kabbalah involves actions that are in conflict with God's will, such as practicing magic and the worship of idols or other gods through the summoning of entities. These practices are seen as violations of God's will and as attempts to attain forbidden knowledge. According to Paul, *"You cannot drink the cup of the Lord and the cup of demons too; you cannot have a part in both the Lord's table and the table of demons. Are we trying to arouse the Lord's jealousy? Are we stronger than he?"* (1 Corinthians 10:21–22, NIV).

Adam Kadmon is the spiritual Adam of Kabbalah. He is thought to contain the blueprint for the Tree of Life, having emerged from the godhead during creation with the same composition of Sephiroth as the original godhead. Some believe him to be the source of all other souls. According to the Lurianic Kabbalah, Adam Kadmon was not strong enough to contain the light within the Sephiroth vessels, which led to the shattering and scattering of their contents throughout the world. Lurianic Kabbalists believe their purpose is to gather this light, referred to as sparks.

From Kabbalistic descriptions of souls and diamonds that I encountered after attempting to research the painting showing a diamond bleeding its brains out, I reasoned that Kabbalists could identify a "divine" woman by looking for a "divine spark" in her eyes, the window into her soul. They search for soulmates with a soul like a raw diamond that can be polished through mental alchemy into a diamond with high-grade versions of the gem-like properties of cut, clarity, color, and carat weight. It seemed the diamond was bleeding out, because it had to surrender its life for the Kabbalist to claim its soul.

These soulmates are thought to contain a holy version of the Sephiroth within them. I questioned whether Kabbalists might use the "divine" souls of women as Sephiroth within their own souls, which they are seeking to perfect. Why else would it be claimed that within each Sephira, all the Sephiroth are contained? Could they be merging with these souls through their magical practices? Is this how they seek union with the unknowable God—by permanently joining with real people who have surrendered their lives?

I watched a video featuring several Kabbalists who described a loving connection with God, achieved through the interaction of the heart chakra, the crown chakra, and the resulting formation of the third eye at the pineal gland. They explained that the heart and crown chakras create a magnetic field that draws God in, which I interpreted as the souls of "divine" women. It appeared that they might use this magnetic pull to integrate these souls into their own oversoul. The oversoul is described as a divine presence connecting life and the universe. Might the oversoul be created from a divine soul as well? According to other literature I encountered, once a soul is reborn into the oversoul of a Kabbalist, it is transformed into a new "creature," lacking memories of its previous life, a body, or a voice. This new entity or "rosebud" becomes like a light within a spherical container guarded by high-level witches. Could this be how the Sephiroth are formed? I interpreted from my reading that these creatures could be kept in a dreamlike state and take on characteristics of the Sephiroth to which they have been assigned. They could be repositioned like pieces on a chessboard, with each move affecting the Kabbalist's experiences.

Another term for chakra is "wheel." There are wheels on the light vehicle called the Merkaba, which is thought by Kabbalists to transport the body and spirit between dimensions and levels of consciousness. The Merkaba is composed of two intersecting tetrahedra rotating in opposite directions. The two form a three-dimensional star. The spirit I was battling was often tinkering with my "wheels" or chakras, preparing to pull my soul from my body. I listened to the spinning sound as they turned; the wheel that would be my crown chakra sounded reminiscent of a computer fan. The idea of listening to my wheels reminded me of the song "Take It Easy" by the Eagles. I wondered, *Do Kabbalists use chakras or wheels to mesmerize women and 'drive them crazy'?*

For a time, while I still felt under a love spell, I focused on the spinning chakras and informed the spirit that I was leaving everything up to God—whether my soul was taken, or I remained in my body to complete my life. I had yet to be introduced to the Scripture that would help me discern God's will for my life, but even then, my will was to do whatever God willed for me. Around this time, my mother's condition began to deteriorate. I overheard demonic voices coming from her, saying to one another, "He could take her soul if she gave him permission." I realized that I needed to move my mind away when I felt the spirit near my chakras. Otherwise, it was as though I was in agreement with the spirit. I did not want to test God, but instead, I desired to make the conscious decision to choose God.

Figure 8 A stylized pink falcon spreads its wings in the air with its claws extended, prepared to grasp. Illuminated gold letters from an unknown language float in the textured pale blue and pink sky. 2017-2018, Pastel and paint on paper

Ecstatic Kabbalah is a form of Kabbalah used to achieve union with the "divine," resulting in mystical experiences and ascension through the attainment of hidden knowledge. "Ecstatic" refers to the otherworldly pleasure experienced during this process. Kabbalah, meaning "to receive," involves the reception and transmission of sexual energy. Practitioners believe this mystical union with the divine is realized through spiritual intercourse and relies on practices that can include ceremonial magic, demonology, mesmerism, meditation, and the study of sacred texts.

Kabbalists employ the practice of vibrating the seventy-two three-letter Hebrew names of God in a prayer-like manner, in conjunction with their chakras. This method is reminiscent of Madonna's song "Like a Prayer," which touches on themes of angels, mysteries, and invoking names as a form of prayer. The vibration of these names is often incorporated into pentagram rituals to summon power or entities that assist in their spiritual journey. Kabbalists believe this practice aligns their energies with the divine and brings them blessings in the form of protection, healing, and the ability to overcome spiritual laws by opening channels of communication to higher spiritual worlds. Many Kabbalists display these divine names on jewelry or place them in their homes. These names are derived from Gematria, a system combining numerology and symbolism, and meditations on Exodus 14:19-21 from the Torah.

Figure 8 was created for my teaching internship using pastels and paint prior to my experience with Kabbalah and depicts a pink falcon flying among floating, golden, sacred letters that remind me of Gematria's magical practices and the visualization of the vibrating letters that make up the seventy-two names of God.

Gematria, as a form of numerology, is considered forbidden because it is a form of divination, which, according to the Bible, is prohibited. The Bible states: *"Let no one be found among you who sacrifices their son or daughter in the fire, practices divination or sorcery, interprets omens, engages in witchcraft, casts spells, consults with mediums or spiritists, or consults the dead. Anyone who does these things is detestable to the Lord; because of these same detestable practices, the Lord your God will drive out those nations before you"* (Deuteronomy 18:10-12, NIV).

Tantra involves meditation practices to connect with the divine through spiritual intercourse, merging physical matter with the mystical. It uses sacred geometry, a system based on shapes and proportions believed to connect the Kabbalist with the energies of the divine. Examples of sacred geometry include the Tree of Life, the Flower of Life, and the Merkaba. These serve as containers to hold the divine. There are two magical paths available when practicing Tantra: the left-hand path, considered evil, and the righthand path, which is based on morality. Kabbalists believe that both paths ultimately lead to the same destination, just as both light and dark are found within the yin-yang symbol. However, according to Scripture, neither path is righteous because they involve the practice of magic and self-will.

Kundalini yoga merges Tantra with yoga practices. Kundalini is described as a feminine energy called Shakti that can be awakened from the base of the spine through yoga. In Kabbalah, Kundalini is used for self-realization, another term for union with God. Yoga can be traced to ancient Sanskrit texts and consists of the Ashtanga or eight-fold path that contains all forms of yoga with the ultimate aim of Samadhi, an ecstatic union with the divine and realization of one's potential. Both Buddhists and Hindus use yoga to seek enlightenment. I wondered about the relationship between enlightenment and union with the divine. Are they the same? Is this why the son of a practicing Kabbalist, who is likely also practicing Kabbalah, is creating artwork featuring the eye of providence on pyramids, which is associated with the Illuminati and enlightenment?

Many Christians view Kundalini Shakti and Shiva as evil forces because they awaken the "serpent power" from the spine on a quest for ascension. This process can be likened to the fall of man when the serpent led Adam and Eve to gain knowledge by partaking of the forbidden fruit from the Tree of Knowledge before they fell from grace.

I believe that allowing the Kundalini spirit to rise is akin to entering into communion with Satan and that any powers experienced are demonic, attained through aligning with this spirit. Once Kundalini was activated in me, an intelligent presence gained access to me. This presence accompanied the buzzing or ringing that I have continued to hear ever since Kundalini rose to my crown chakra. The only times this buzzing stopped were when the spirit exited. The serpent power climbed my chakras, activating them, and ever since I have been able to feel the touch of invisible forces in the spiritual realm. I have felt demons crawling on me and in me and have borne witness to their intrusive thoughts. I have experienced disturbing encounters with invisible spirits and a wide variety of phenomena. It is thought that Kundalini accesses the central nervous system and can cause a range of physical sensations.

Just as Satan tempted Jesus with a kingdom, I believe he entices individuals to practice Kabbalah by promising hidden wisdom and power. Ritual magic and meditation, even if not consciously recognized as prayers to Satan, can manipulate other individuals, making them vulnerable. The Kabbalists may use their practices to mesmerize or hypnotize others, similar to how a spider ensnares its prey. Overwhelmed with bliss and dulled senses, individuals may not resist until it is too late. Under magical influence, they may struggle to seek help and spiritual guidance, risking their souls or lives if not rescued by God's grace. I believe once the Kabbalists have gathered these souls, they begin a process of transformation, using the individual souls to create one perfected soul. This may help explain the grown men born to virgin women shown in Renaissance art, where a divine figure holds a perfect child resembling an adult male.

To become like a god, Kabbalists engage in alchemy to complete their "Great Work" or "Magnum Opus." This spiritual process involves transforming prima materia into the philosopher's stone. The Alchemist must balance elements and energies within themselves, with the feminine power symbolized by the moon, water, and mercury and the masculine power symbolized by the sun, secret fire, and sulfur. The stages of purification include nigredo (blackening), peacock stage (iridescence), albedo (whitening), citrinitas (yellowing), and rubedo (reddening), with the final stage producing the philosopher's stone, which generates gold and the elixir of life, signifying the perfected, immortal soul.

With a perfected soul, I have read that the Kabbalist will be able to enter Heaven and seek enlightenment, wearing the "white garment" of virgin spirits or Sephiroth as he approaches the gateway of Heaven. He will pray to God for enlightenment, and once received, he may choose to cast out the spirits of those with whom he merged. It may be that they were deceived, and their heavenly crowns were replaced with the illusion of crystalline crowns that masked demonic presence and enabled mind control that caused them to turn away from God and surrender their lives.

Chapter 9

The Garden

When the serpent spoke to Eve in the Garden of Eden, she was deceived into questioning God's commands. God had told her not to eat the fruit of the Tree of Knowledge, but the serpent caused her to doubt what God had said. He tempted her with the possibility of becoming like God by having the same knowledge as God. Eve tasted the fruit and offered it to Adam, who also ate it. This act led to the original sin, resulting in the inequity of the human race. The serpent continues to tempt us.

In a similar way, it is my belief that the serpent tempts Kabbalists to partake in what they call the Tree of Life, but in reality, they are consuming from the Tree of Knowledge. They are deceived into viewing Jesus not as our God but as a guide toward what can be perceived as unrighteousness. Seeking to become like gods themselves rather than following the God who created us and gave us commandments, they are enticed by the promise of hidden knowledge and enlightenment. They believe that by constructing their own Tree of Life and completing the Great Work, they will attain god-like power within their own microcosm.

Likewise, it seems Kabbalists may use the Kundalini serpent or another form of spiritual intercourse to tempt individuals, encouraging them to seek adulterous, sexual bliss and to believe that they will become like divine goddesses. They are deceived, and these choices lead to destruction and death.

Shield

I sat on a swing set and apologized to God for committing adultery with a spirit and for not being devoted to my husband, whom I am blessed to have. I prayed to God to provide me with a shield to stop the spirits from violating me any longer. Immediately, God answered my prayer. I felt a shield appear, and the touching stopped. For a moment, I thought it was all over. The buzzing instantly grew faint, but I still felt intense love in my heart for the spirit, so I walked through a nearby field, saying my goodbyes. As I did this, the unclean spirit grew in strength, and I was afflicted once again. My affection had granted the spirit permission to stay. God will help us fight our enemies, but first, we need to recognize Satan's spirits as our enemies. Only then, *"The Lord will grant that the enemies who rise up against you will be defeated before you. They will come at you from one direction but flee from you in seven."* (Deuteronomy 28:7, NIV).

I decided to follow the advice of the lightworker and reached out to the blacksmith via text, intending to ask him to end this nightmarish connection. I asked him why I liked him so much, and he responded, "What are you wearing?" When I inquired if he felt what I felt, he confirmed that he did. I told him I wanted this to end, and he mentioned that the heat sometimes turns people away and that he thought I wanted to change the nature of this relationship. I hoped this conversation would bring it all to an end.

As I stood by the kitchen table, I felt the spirit leave me, and I was ecstatic when the buzzing stopped. However, my joy soon turned to sadness. I felt empty, cold, and alone. The pain was intense, and I wondered how I could endure it. Moments later, the spirit seemed to return as if it had never left. That night, as I lay in bed, it felt as if the spirit of death enveloped me, blowing around me with great force. Eventually, it left, and I felt some relief. I told my mother about it in the morning, and she explained that the spirit might have been an angel assigned to claim me. She said the angel could not affect me without permission from God.

I continued to struggle with the spirit or spirits over the next days and weeks. I was uncertain whether I was dealing with a demon, an astral body, or a fragment of someone's soul. I had read that just as it takes a diamond to cut a diamond, only another soul can affect a soul, and I wondered if this person had sent a part of their soul to harm me. I tried to resist by focusing my mind away from the sensations I felt and distracting myself by wiggling my feet or pinching myself. At times, I succeeded in diverting my thoughts and falling asleep, but often I was awakened at 3 AM by a spirit poking me. I felt overwhelmed and sometimes gave in to the sensations. During one instance, the spirit whispered into my ear, "I love adulterous sex."

I then realized that I was dealing with a demonic spirit rather than the loving spirit of a man. There was no divine love here, and it was contrary to what God commands in Exodus 20:14 (NIV), *"Thou shalt not commit adultery."* At that moment, I knew I could no longer engage with this spirit, regardless of whether it could perceive my thoughts.

Cackling

One evening, when my husband came to bed, something seemed to have come over him. He was not himself; he acted out angrily and spoke crudely. His actions and words were wicked and unclean. I did not know what to do, so I left the room, desperate to escape him. I navigated through the hoarded mess in my father's room, trying to find a place to lay down for the night. There was no place to rest. As I sat among the boxes, feeling broken and defeated, I heard the very real cackle of witches echoing through my mind. It became apparent that my husband was the victim of witchcraft, and I realized I had to forgive him rather than let the situation destroy our marriage.

Later, I messaged the blacksmith again, asking him to end this connection. When he responded, he assumed I had already left my husband and needed a place to stay. How did he know we were struggling unless he was aware of the witchcraft involved? I informed him that I was committed to my husband and did not need a place to stay. This seemed to relieve the blacksmith, which I believe was because he was housing the other woman who had been writing on social media about separating from her husband and seeking true love. She shared photos of her son taking private lessons with the blacksmith. That night, the spirit that seemed like death revisited me, passing over me as before.

When the full moon arrived, I remembered the lightworker and gathered every object I could find from the blacksmith's shop, including a coffee mug that my son had received. I searched everywhere for it and finally located it under my son's bed. It was strange how what I now believed to be a cursed object could conceal itself so well. I was nervous. Something told me that this was not right, but I had committed to going through with the ritual. Other women might depend on me binding this man. I reviewed the words that I was to recite, given to me by the lightworker. Nothing mentioned the spirits of the cardinal directions, so I decided this ritual might not be a spell and it was safe for me to perform it.

Moments after I lit the flame, my phone alerted me to a new message. The blacksmith had texted a mysterious verse, which I cannot fully remember, but it was something about servant, fire, and master. How did he know? The spirits he sent to assault me must have informed him, or maybe he was reading my mind, or maybe he was a demon himself. What did he mean by a servant? Servant of God? This made no sense to me. I never considered myself a servant, but if I was a servant of God, I definitely should not have lit that fire.

I wanted to share what I had learned about Kabbalah with the lightworker who had tried to help me earlier. I wanted her to understand that all forms of magic, whether labeled as light or dark, are powered by the same source: the souls of women deceived into becoming Sephiroth in the Tree Life, the spirits of the cardinal directions, and that all magic ultimately comes from Satan, including divination. The lightworker responded to my message, saying she had a friend who reads tarot cards and would do a reading for me. They had remotely scanned my energy and found a blockage in my throat chakra, which had cleared. I thought this must have been when I felt choking. I told her that I had discovered tarot cards were of Satan, but she did not want to accept this. Despite this, she acknowledged that her friend's husband had heard a discussion about Sephiroth from other men and could confirm some of what I had said.

A man I met in a Kabbalah chat online confirmed my understanding. I expressed my frustration about men stealing the souls of women and then discarding them. He was surprised to be talking to someone going through this and suggested that my marital problems might be to blame. He shared several photos and connected the concept of men consuming the souls and discarding the spirits of women to the ouroboros, the serpent that consumes itself. He justified this by saying that men worship women in this life, I assume he meant the Goddess, and it is only fair that the next life is built around them. He also mentioned putting the cart before the ass, seemingly to indicate things being done out of order. I expressed my desire for this to end, and he suggested that I change my frequency, saying that men usually find a way to worm into actualization eventually. I asked how to change my frequency, and the conversation ended. He must have realized I was the prey and he was the predator, revealing too much.

I shared my story with my mother-in-law, telling her that I believed men were stealing the souls of women to perfect their own and sneak into Heaven for enlightenment. She corrected me, reminding me that God knows all things. No one can deceive God, even though men practicing Kabbalah might believe they can. *They perish because they [refuse] to love the truth and so be saved. For this reason God sends them a powerful delusion so that they will believe the lie and so that all will be condemned who have not believed the truth but have delighted in wickedness"* (2 Thessalonians 2: 10-12, NIV). I showed her the text messages from the blacksmith. She noticed that when I asked for help, he had advised me to turn away and spoke in riddles. She thought this might mean I needed to revisit the memory of the event and change how I reacted to it.

Later that night, she sent me Reiki energy without warning, and I felt it. It felt the same as the demonic energy sent to me by the spirit I was battling. When I spoke to her again, she told me she was channeling energy to me, but I had been resisting it. I told her I did not want to receive any more Reiki energy, certain that it came from the Sephiroth deceived by Satan. The following night, my father-inlaw prayed for me. I saw him while lying in bed, trying to sleep. He took my hand while wearing a white robe, and we floated up into the sky, past the earth, and out into the universe. I pulled away before we went any further because I was afraid of straying too far from earth.

I followed my mother-in-law's advice and imagined going back in time to the moment when this all began. This time, I turned away from the blacksmith when he first put his elbow on my chest. I rehearsed this like a dance, reenacting it over and over with my body and mind, hoping to reverse the entire process. I remembered that the lightworker had advised me to punch or kick him, thinking he was pretending to be a snake inside of me. I decided to attack the blacksmith by visualizing myself coming at him. Nothing changed, so I decided to go back even further in my imagination. I envisioned the destruction of all his ancestors, every Kabbalist, and all the energies connecting them. We battled. Later, I learned I needed to find forgiveness to be healed.

Chapter 10

God Answers Prayers

Prayer

In March 2020, an old friend messaged me to ask my take on whether COVID-19 was a plan of the New World Order. I did not mention what I was going through but shared what my mother had said: "Only people who are not covenant," were being destroyed. Only a few days later, my father passed away in the hospital. I had been so absorbed in my own issues that I had not even realized he was dying.

He had been admitted to the hospital several weeks earlier for a UTI that had spread throughout his body as a staph infection, but I was sure he would pull through under the hospital's care. We lost regular contact because new restrictions at the hospital prevented my sister and me from seeing him daily. I was devastated when I found out they had not even told my dad that they were not allowing us in to visit him. I had been coming every day, but then, one day, they stopped me and assured me that the patients knew we were restricted from visiting due to COVID-19. About a week later, my dad had a nurse help him call me, wondering why we had stopped coming to see him. My heart broke that he went all that time without knowing why we had not come.

Mini strokes had affected his vision, and he was not able to answer his cell phone. We tried to call every few days, but it was difficult to get through because he was in a room without a phone, and the nurses seldom answered. I received a call from my dad's doctor on the day he died, informing me my dad had suffered a heart attack and asking whether to resuscitate him if it happened again. Of course, I agreed, but my father could not be saved. He suffered another heart attack within the next couple of hours.

The doctor told me that earlier in the day, my father had complained about chest pain. The doctor did not treat it because medication for his heart would have caused additional complications since he was also being treated for strokes. I was not included in that decision, but I am not sure if a better choice could have been made. I was barely able to grieve. Everything felt so unreal. I am grateful that God allowed me to grieve for my father before I went to Spain.

It was sometime in October when I reached out to my friend and shared what I was experiencing. I told him that I believed a Kabbalist was trying to take my soul through mesmerism. Kabbalists, I explained, take women as spirit brides to use as Sephiroth in their Tree of Life, absorbing their virtues and then discarding their spirits in a final stage of alchemy while seeking enlightenment. I mentioned that they use prayers similar to one I had come across, requesting that those betrothed to the condensate be cast out as refuse. I told my friend that the women are attacked through their chakras, but because they have been hypnotized, they are unable to speak about what they are experiencing.

My friend is a spiritual man, and after I shared my troubles with him, he put me in touch with his friend, who is a pastor. I called the pastor and his wife that day or the next, and they invited me to a virtual prayer meeting. Through intercession, a large group of Pentecostal prayer warriors on Zoom prayed for me. I followed their lead and prayed a prayer of repentance and acceptance of God. They called out, praising the Lord, and the Lord revealed many of my sins to them. They spoke of unforgiveness, tarot cards, crystals in the walls, unclean spirits in my bed, an unclean spirit that had been with me since childhood, and they told me to stop my imagination. My imagination? This must have meant all the meditation and visualizations I had been doing.

I felt my body shake as they prayed, hoping the spirit would leave, but it never came out. A stronghold of some kind still held me captive. After the prayers, I slept better. I had hope in Jesus and a new understanding of how Jesus died for me, paid the price for my sins, rose three days later, and defeated death. The battle was not over, but now I knew where to begin, and that was with prayer and repentance.

How could I have forgotten God? Why did I run toward witchcraft instead of God? Didn't I learn my lesson when I decided never to cast another spell? I had so much regret and felt so filthy. I am a sinner and have been a sinner all my life, but I thought I was good. I was always making sacrifices to help others. How could an unclean spirit have gained access to me in childhood? My relative baptized me. Did my relatives who were involved with the Freemasons curse me? Was I cursed? Did the spells I cast as a teenager result in curses on my life? Were generational curses afflicting my family in the past, present, and future?

I began praying daily and even hourly. I wanted nothing more than to be set free. The pastor and his wife guided me to books on deliverance, and I purged my house of every object that could be accursed. I destroyed pictures, books, jewelry, decorative objects, stamp collections, my art, others' art, report cards, achievement awards, playing cards, messages, writings, and so much more. No object was safe. I wanted to rid my family and myself of any object that might be offensive to God and a gateway allowing the enemy in.

I began reading the Bible, listening to online sermons, and seeking out deliverance classes. The Bible was difficult for me to decipher without help. I was confused by the language, which I had seen used in different contexts when I was learning about Kabbalah. I had uncertainty about my ability to discern the true intentions of God. What does the Bible mean by "one flesh"? What does the Bible mean by "mystery"? The enemy used my fears, doubts, and exposure to Satan's lies against me. He had twisted the meaning of Scripture through the teachings of Kabbalah, but slowly, as my understanding of Scripture grew, my faith grew with it. I learned that Satan is *"The great dragon … hurled down—that ancient serpent called the devil, or Satan, who leads the whole world astray. He was hurled to the earth, and his angels with him,"* and has taken what is holy and created counterfeits (Revelation 12:9, NIV). Those who believe that Scripture supports Kabbalah and that Satan is God's right-hand man have been deceived by the false god they worship, Satan.

Churches were still shut down due to COVID-19, but the sermons given by online pastors inspired me. I understood that *"We wrestle not against flesh and blood, but against principalities, against powers, against the rulers of the darkness of this world, against spiritual wickedness in high places"* (Ephesians 6:12, NIV). I was not battling this man; I was battling Satan. The Kabbalists are men who have become like demons, deceived by Satan, just as I had been deceived. Satan tempted them, and they believed his lie that they could deceive God and become like gods themselves. I learned that I was not fighting a physical battle but a spiritual one, and I could not win this battle by shielding my body with protective clothing or jewelry or by attempting to distract myself from physical symptoms. To win this spiritual battle, I need to put on the full armor of God and build my faith in Jesus (Ephesians 6:10-18).

Over the weeks and months that followed, I became more familiar with Scripture and worked through my internal struggles in understanding God's Word. I felt guilt and frustration that I was raised in a house without knowledge of God's Gospel. I wondered how my life would have been different if I had known God's Word. Could I have avoided all of this? Should I have avoided all of this? I believe that God is using me to share what I have experienced to help others. This would not be possible if events in my life had worked out differently. If I had never been afflicted, I would never have learned about the wicked works of the enemy that I encountered. I assumed life must be easier for those raised as Christians, but after listening to numerous testimonies, I now know it is not. Many rebel against the very God who died to save us, and some never humble themselves and come back to Him.

I worked through my doubts and made peace with my enemies and with myself because, *"Do not judge, and you will not be judged. Do not condemn, and you will not be condemned. Forgive, and you will be forgiven"* (Luke 6:37, NIV). We must *"Love [our] enemies and pray for those who persecute [us]"* (Matthew 5:44, NIV). I confessed my sins and repented over and over. I repented of every wicked thing I could remember doing and rebuked all of them in the name of Jesus. I prayed for forgiveness and cleansing and found assurance in knowing that *"If we confess our sins, he is faithful and just and will forgive us our sins and purify us from all unrighteousness"* (1 John 1:9, NIV).

I had opened what seemed like countless gateways for the enemy to enter throughout my lifetime. I cried when I read how God's anger burned against the Israelites when they grumbled about the manna they were given to eat in the desert because I was no better (Numbers 11:1-34). I might have grumbled if I had been there. I wondered how God could love me, but I learned that God does love me. He has a plan: *"For God so loved the world that He gave His only begotten Son, that whosoever believeth in Him should not perish, but have everlasting life"* (John 3:16, NIV). God knew that I would sin and had already paid the price for me so that my sins could be forgiven. I am washed clean because *"If we walk in the light, as he is in the light, we have fellowship with one another, and the blood of Jesus, his Son, purifies us from all sin"* (1 John 1:7, NIV).

I have been working toward moving closer to God through prayer and fasting, but I am not immune to making mistakes along the way. I attempted to speak in tongues, as referenced in Scripture, because I have heard many people of faith say that prayer language will help your prayer life grow stronger. However, I found that the utterances I made were anything but unintelligible. After researching each of the words that came to me individually, I discovered that my prayer language had been hijacked by the enemy spirit that I am still battling.

The final prayer in tongues that I spoke is, "Masta rishma tore mahore ryna," and I translated this to mean, "Master, beam of light, tear the price paid for the bride, melted." The enemy knows that I will not be a bride of Satan or any Kabbalist. I choose Jesus as my Lord and Savior. Another prayer in tongues that I translated is, "Master, I am stupid. Help me give up my will to the infinite." I have been humbled but have no intention of giving up my will. My will is my identity. It is my desire to exist, and I am blessed to exist. In no way do I intend to give up what God has blessed me with, unlike Esau, who gave up his birthright for a bowl of soup. I will not give up my soul for the illusion of love. I love my life and my God, who blessed me with it.

Regardless of the enemy's tricks, if we have faith in Jesus, we will be well because *"You, dear children, are from God and have overcome them, because the one who is in you is greater than the one who is in the world"* (1 John 4:4, NIV).

The Victory Belongs to Jesus

My struggle is not over, but the battle has already been won: *"For everyone born of God overcomes the world. This is the victory that has overcome the world, even our faith. Who is it that overcomes the world? Only the one who believes that Jesus is the Son of God"* (1 John 5:4-5, NIV). Most days, I am well, and I no longer feel internal touch from spirits of the kingdom of darkness, but I know that if I do, I just need to keep my trust in Jesus. Each time I do, I am made well. The enemy uses strongholds over our minds to convince us that there is no hope. When I sufficiently strengthen my faith in God, the enemy will pass. I am battling demons, and I know when the time is right, they will be cast out in the name of Jesus from me forever. For now, they serve as a thorn in my side to remind me that the battle for our souls is real.

We have no need to fear. Fear will give power and authority over our lives to the enemy. Instead, we need to be steadfast in our prayer, faith, and knowledge of God's Word. God speaks to us through His Word, often through a thought, a dream, or an image. If we do not have knowledge of God's Word, we cannot fully receive His guidance. Reading the Bible and staying in God's Word is critical for His people. Otherwise, we can be easily deceived by the serpent or even by well-meaning people who twist Scripture to suit their own purpose.

It is important to guard our minds from the works of the enemy, which can come in many forms, including literature and music. Even after I had been well for so long, I felt the spirit enter me again while researching to write this book. The spirit entered because I was open to it by exposing myself to a video about alchemical symbolism. We need to put on the full armor of God and plead the blood of Jesus over our homes and minds daily. I recognize the enemy's spirit now because I have been battling it for so long. The spirit I have been fighting only has one bag of tricks, all of which involve creating the illusion of touch by manipulating the nervous system. It took me a day to get myself back together and remember that Satan has no authority over God's people.

Satan is a deceiver and will take any power given to him. You might assume he has the authority to do what he does, but he does not, as long as you are in good standing with God. Our faith is tested, and our knowledge of Scripture is our sword. If there are unrepented sins giving Satan legal access to our lives, deliverance can be achieved through prayer, repentance, living according to God's Word, and avoiding sinful objects and activities. After praying, the sensations stopped again, and I consider myself well. I am well in spirit as long as my faith in my Heavenly Father is strong. I know that the unclean spirit has not left my soul yet, evident by the satanic buzzing, but the physical assaults have ceased. I pray to God daily for deliverance, and I believe that it will come in God's time, not mine. My job is to keep faith in Jesus and to share God's Word with you. Do not let others tell you that you cannot be saved. God's grace is sufficient (Corinthians 12:9).

As long as we have breath, we have time to choose Jesus Christ as our Lord and Savior. It is not too late. All who are saved are blessed, *"But many who are first will be last, and many who are last will be first"* (Matthew 19:30, NIV). God loves you. If you are not yet saved, you can be saved now because *"If you declare with your mouth, 'Jesus is Lord,' and believe in your heart that God raised him from the dead, you will be saved. For it is with your heart that you believe and are justified, and it is with your mouth that you profess your faith and are saved"* (Romans 10:9-10, NIV).